Edmund Fitzgerald

The Legendary Great Lakes Shipwreck

Elle Andra-Warner

North Shore Press
Grand Marais, MN

River Rocks Publishing
Thunder Bay, Ontario

U.S. Publisher
North Shore Press
A division of
Northern Wilds Media, Inc.
PO Box 26, Grand Marais, MN 55604
(218) 387-9475
www.NorthernWilds.com

ISBN 0-9740207-3-7

Canadian Publisher
River Rocks Publishing
331-1100 Memorial Ave.
Thunder Bay, Ontario
www.RiverRocks.ca

Library and Archives Canada Cataloguing in Publication

Andra-Warner, Elle, 1946-
Edmund Fitzgerald : The Legendary Great Lakes Shipwreck
Elle Andra-Warner.

ISBN 978-0-9782721-4-2

1. Edmund Fitzgerald (Ship). 2. Shipwrecks--Superior, Lake.
I. Title.

G530.E26W36 2009   917.74'90443   C2009-902739-9

Printed in Canada by Friesens Printing

10 9 8 7 6 5 4

To all the mariners who have sailed the Great Lakes

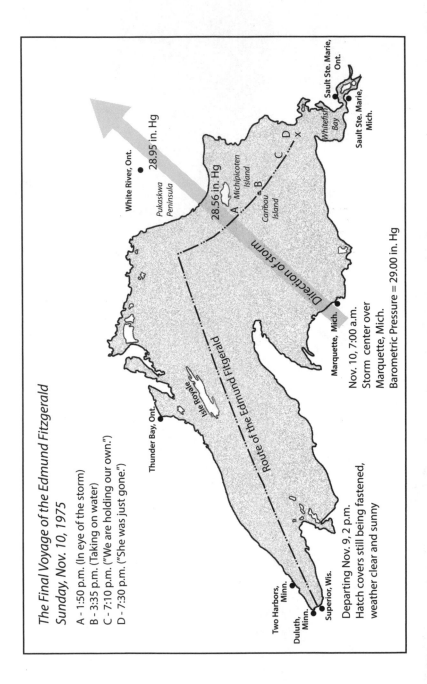

The Final Voyage of the Edmund Fitzgerald
Sunday, Nov. 10, 1975

A - 1:50 p.m. (In eye of the storm)
B - 3:35 p.m. (Taking on water)
C - 7:10 p.m. ("We are holding our own.")
D - 7:30 p.m. ("She was just gone.")

Departing Nov. 9, 2 p.m.
Hatch covers still being fastened,
weather clear and sunny

Nov. 10, 7:00 a.m.
Storm center over
Marquette, Mich.
Barometric Pressure = 29.00 in. Hg

Direction of storm

28.95 in. Hg

28.56 in. Hg

Route of the Edmund Fitzgerald

White River, Ont.

Pukaskwa Peninsula

Michipicoten Island

Caribou Island

Sault Ste. Marie, Ont.

Sault Ste. Marie, Mich.

Whitefish Bay

Marquette, Mich.

Isle Royale

Thunder Bay, Ont.

Two Harbors, Minn.

Duluth, Minn.

Superior, Wis.

6

Contents

Prologue

On November 10, 1975, Dr. Charlie Frederick was an assistant professor at the University of Minnesota in Duluth. He was also a songwriter/musician. Within hours of hearing the *Edmund Fitzgerald* was lost in a storm, he began writing the first song ever written about the *Fitzgerald* tragedy, "Twenty-Nine More Men."

On a cold windy November night
The Fitz with iron aboard
Without a know'in of a vicious storm blow'in'
On the Great Lakes of the north
Thirty-foot waves blown by violent wind
Took the iron ore boat they say
And twenty-nine more men went down in a cold
deep grave.

According to the TV newsmen
Another ore boat was tailin' Fitz
Near Sault Saint Marie on a stormy sea
The Great Lakes storm they hit
Seemed in mind just a flash of time
The Fitz passed out of sight
And twenty-nine more men lost their lives that night.

CHORUS
Great Lakes storms are wild and mean
They've conquered man before
Of all the lakes the ones that takes
Are the Great Lakes of the north
Duluth in the north to the Eastern Port
Many people will remember the fright
When twenty-nine more men lost their lives that
night.

For three long days and weary nights
The search was underway
To find the boat and men afloat
The loved ones hoped and prayed
Search crew said Fitz came apart
Ninety fathoms the pieces were found
And twenty-nine more men the Great Lakes have
taken down.

Reprinted with the permission of Dr. Charlie Frederick
and Charlie Frederick Music Enterprises.

I
The *Fitzgerald* Dynasty

Some sailors believe that a ship's name is its soul, and that it's bad luck to name a vessel after one that has gone down. If this is indeed the case, then the legendary lake freighter *Edmund Fitzgerald* — which sank in Lake Superior on November 10, 1975 — was doomed 75 years before she was even launched.

The First Fitzgerald

The story of the *Edmund Fitzgerald* has its roots in the small Irish parish of Oola, in County Limerick, where, on November 13, 1817, William Fitzgerald married Julianna (Julia) Real. Eighteen years later, the couple decided to move to North America, and on January 25, 1836, they arrived in New York City on the sailing ship *Mount Zion* with their nine children in tow.

Originally, William and Julianna had been headed for Canada, but after living for a time in New York, they settled down to farm and to raise their children (now numbering 12) along the banks of the St. Clair River in Michigan's East China Township. Running between Lake Huron and Lake St. Clair, the St. Clair River was a major commercial shipping channel, providing access to all the ports along the Great Lakes. As the

Fitzgerald children grew up, the six boys began to feel the pull of the water, and each of them went on to captain Great Lakes schooners.

The eldest Fitzgerald son, Edmond, was the first to surrender to the lure of the Great Lakes. Already a young man when he moved to the United States with his parents and siblings, he had gone to live on his own in nearby Port Huron soon after their arrival. After working for a while in lumbering, he took to the lakes, eventually becoming master of such schooners as the *Hard Times*, the *J. B. Skinner*, the *Gulielma*, and the *Oneida Chief*.

When Edmond stopped sailing in 1866, he became a shipbuilder in Port Huron, and his shipyard stretched for 600 feet along the St. Clair River. In 1870, he and his partners at Fitzgerald & Leichford built a two-masted, 134-foot schooner that he named the *E. Fitzgerald*. On her first trip, the new schooner delivered a load of lumber from Port Huron to Buffalo.

In 1873, Edmond began to shift his focus from building ships to investing in them. He also entered politics in Port Huron, serving first as an alderman for four terms in the 1870s, and then as mayor from 1879 to 1880. In October 1883, the Fitzgerald shipyard disappeared from Great Lakes marine history when Edmond closed the business and sold the property. Within a month, his namesake schooner, the *E. Fitzgerald* (now owned by a man from Buffalo), met a tragic end.

On November 14, 1883, the *E. Fitzgerald* was sailing on Lake Erie, headed for Buffalo with a load of wheat from Detroit. The schooner, manned by a crew of six to eight, was commanded by 31-year-old Captain Dan Langdon, the youngest of three brothers who were all Great Lakes captains.

A ferocious snowstorm suddenly materialized and swept across Lake Erie, wrecking the E. *Fitzgerald* near Long Point, just 300 yards from the lake's northern shore. Rescuers from the life-saving station at the nearby town of Port Rowan, Ontario, raced into action. But before they could launch their lifeboat, the *Fitzgerald's* crew had lowered the ship's yawl into the stormy sea, piled into it, and headed for shore.

About a third of the distance to shore, the crew lost control of the boat in the rough water. Suddenly, a wave slammed the yawl broadside, swamping it and throwing everyone overboard. People along the north shore watched helplessly as the crew struggled and then disappeared beneath the water's surface. There was brief hope for at least one survivor when a crewmember managed to grab an oar, but the strong undertow soon carried him away to his death, just as it had with the others.

By morning, the wrecked E. *Fitzgerald* looked like a mass of solid ice. With the seas still too rough for anyone to get to the ship, rescuers on the beach were forced to peer through a telescope to confirm the ship's identity. Meanwhile, there was no doubt that the whole crew, including the captain, was dead.

The demise of the 13-year-old E. *Fitzgerald* was big news in 1883. As newspapers reported what limited details they could, the ship's owner went out to visit the wreck. He quickly blamed the crew for the loss of their lives, suggesting they would have been saved if they had climbed onto the ship's rigging and waited for rescue instead of taking to the yawl.

Then, to add to the shipwreck controversy, on November 20 the Buffalo Commercial Advertiser reported that a tug owned by a Mr. Hickler of Buffalo had been in the vicinity of the wrecked vessel but could not go to the rescue of the crew, "owing to the absurd regulations of the Canadian government concerning wrecking under which [Hickler's] tug would have been liable to seizure, if he had offered assistance."

The Next Two Ships

Four years after the sinking of the *E. Fitzgerald*, another Fitzgerald vessel began to sail the Great Lakes. She was the *R. P. Fitzgerald*, a 271-foot steamer named for the third of the six Fitzgerald brothers, Robert Patrick Fitzgerald.

Built by the Detroit Shipbuilding Company for a rumoured cost of $130,000, the *R. P. Fitzgerald* was one of four ships belonging to the Milwaukee Steamship Company's White Fleet, which was owned by Robert Fitzgerald and his two partners, W. P. Egan and P. Armour. On September 5, 1887, the Milwaukee Sentinel reported on the ship's inaugural voyage, calling her "one of the finest steamships on the lakes."

Nearly 20 years after the launching of the *R. P. Fitzgerald*, a third ship carrying the Fitzgerald family name was built for the Chicago Navigation Company. Christened the *W. E. Fitzgerald*, she was named after William Edmund Fitzgerald, son of Captain John Fitzgerald, the youngest of the seafaring Fitzgerald brothers.

Following his sailing career, John Fitzgerald became a prominent Milwaukee businessman, building and repairing ships through his two companies, Milwaukee Ship Yards Inc. and the Milwaukee Dry Dock Company. When John died in 1896, his son William took over his business (by then, only the Milwaukee Dry Dock Co. still existed). Three years later, William merged the company with several other Great Lakes shipyards to form the American Shipbuilding Company.

The first general manager of the new company was William himself, but his role was short-lived. In 1901, the 52-year-old businessman died after a gas generator exploded in the basement of his summer home on Lake Nagawicka, near Milwaukee. His Ontario-born widow, Jesse Blackburn Fitzgerald, was left to raise their two children—William Lennox and Edmund—alone.

In 1906, five years after William's death, the 440-foot-long steel-hulled bulk freighter *W. E. Fitzgerald* was built in his honour by the Detroit Shipbuilding Company. Considered small by lake standards, the freighter had a triple-expansion engine powered with steam from two Scotch boilers.

For the next 12 years, the *R. P. Fitzgerald* and the *W. E. Fitzgerald* continued to ply the Great Lakes. Then, on October 3, 1918, the barge *Grampion* ran into the *R. P. Fitzgerald* at the dock of the Northern Navigation Company. As the Marine Review later reported, "The *Fitzgerald* was damaged so seriously that she sank in 22 feet of water directly in front of the coal dock. Capt. T. Eming ... considers her a total loss." The once grand steamer was abandoned on the Pine River and left to disintegrate.

Eight years later, in 1926, the *W. E. Fitzgerald* nearly met her own end after she sailed around the dangerous Whitefish

Point in Lake Superior and ran into a fierce winter storm that covered all of Whitefish Bay. The freighter battled extreme blizzard conditions for three days as she headed toward the Soo Locks at Sault Ste. Marie, Michigan. She struggled to stay afloat as she was battered by huge, icy waves, whipped up by heavy southeast winds. By the time she arrived at the locks, she was covered with more than 250 tons of ice and looked very much like a ghost ship. Fortunately, she and her crew recovered from the ordeal.

The following year, the *W. E. Fitzgerald* was working on the Great Lakes once again. As a bulk freighter, she primarily hauled sand, coal, and crushed stone. Converted in 1928 to a scraper-type self-unloader, she continued to sail the Great Lakes until she was sold in the late 1960s to the American Steamship Company (who did not put her into service).

In 1971, the *W. E. Fitzgerald* was sold again, this time to the Marine Salvage Company at Port Colborne, Ontario. In October of that year, the 65-year-old freighter took her last journey. Two Canadian tugs, the *Herbert A* and the *G. W. Roger*, brought her up to Humberstone, Ontario, where she was dismantled during the winter of 1971–72. Pieces of the historic vessel were given to William Edmund Fitzgerald's son, Edmund, who donated the ship's nameboard to the Wisconsin Marine Historical Society, and the compass to the Manitowoc Maritime Museum.

The Biggest and Fastest Fitzgerald

In 1957, 14 years before the *W. E. Fitzgerald* was scrapped, the Northwestern Mutual Life Insurance Company (NMLIC)

The 440-foot-long steel-hulled bulk freighter W. E. Fitzgerald, built in 1906. (C. Patrick Labadie Collection, Lake Superior Maritime Collections, UW-Superior)

made headline news when it announced that it was going to build the largest and fastest freshwater freighter ever to be launched on the Great Lakes. NMLIC would maintain ownership of the vessel, but would place it on a 25-year renewable lease to the Columbia Transportation Division of Cleveland's Oglebay Norton Company.

The president of NMLIC at the time was Edmund Fitzgerald (the son of William Edmund Fitzgerald and grandson of Captain John Fitzgerald). Although Edmund had never worked as a mariner, he loved the Great Lakes and had always enjoyed his summer excursions on lake freighters. His nostalgia for the lakes, however, was balanced by strong business acumen — he saw the Great Lakes as a crucial link between resources in the American Midwest and the industrial sectors in the east. Under his leadership, NMLIC had become the single largest investor in companies operating on the Great Lakes and St. Lawrence Seaway. Financing the building of its own ships was a logical next step for NMLIC, particularly as it geared up to celebrate its 100-year anniversary.

In April 1958, a few months before the ship's launch, Edmund Fitzgerald stepped down as president of NMLIC and took on the role of chair of the company's board of trustees. In recognition of his years of company service and his strong family history in Great Lakes shipping, the trustees proposed naming their new ship the *Edmund Fitzgerald*. Edmund opposed the idea and suggested several other names for the ship, including the *Centennial, Seaway, Milwaukee,* and *Northwestern*.

But the other board members were not swayed. They rejected Edmund's suggestions and voted unanimously to name the ship for him. Besides, they told him, it was a long-held Great Lakes tradition to name ships after the senior executives of the companies that built or owned them. Still, as board trustee Louis Quarles later noted, "It was with the greatest difficulty that we got Ed to consent to the use of his name on the ship."

It took about 1000 men to build Hull #301 (as the ship was referred to before being named), at a cost of $8.4 million. She was the first vessel to be built in a revolutionary new manner. Usually ships were constructed in one piece from the keel up, but the *Edmund Fitzgerald* was built in pieces, with large sections of the hull each weighing as much as 70 tons. These prefabricated pieces were then lifted into place by heavy mobile cranes.

Designed and constructed by Great Lakes Engineering Works in River Rouge, Michigan, the *Edmund Fitzgerald* weighed 13,632 tons and measured 729 feet long, 39 feet tall, and 75 feet wide. Her rudder alone weighed 23 tons, and she had a four-blade bronze propeller that measured 19.5 feet in diameter. Powered by a Westinghouse steam turbine with 7500 horsepower and 284-ton coal-burning boilers (later converted to oil-fired), she was to be one of the fastest ships on the Great Lakes, with a top speed of around 18 miles per hour.

The *Edmund Fitzgerald* was built to carry taconite (low-grade iron ore) pellets from northern Minnesota to Detroit — a 750-mile journey. The taconite was loaded onto the ship through chutes that led to an area the height of a three-story building. At full cargo, the *Fitzgerald* could carry enough taconite to the steel mills to build 7500 cars.

The ship's launch on Saturday, June 8, 1958, was a big event in Detroit. Over 15,000 people were in attendance, including Edmund Fitzgerald himself and several members of his family. As the crowd gathered, military planes, commercial airliners, and helicopters flew overhead, while on the Detroit River, a flotilla of boats — yachts, sailboats, fishing boats, tugs, scows, and freighters — waited to welcome the new ship. Among these vessels was the 32-year-old *W. E. Fitzgerald*, which saluted the new *Fitzgerald* by blasting her deep horn.

Edmund Fitzgerald's wife, Elizabeth, was given the honour of christening the ship. Looking regal in a dark blue dress, white gloves, and a white pillbox hat, she said, "I christen you *Edmund Fitzgerald*... God bless you," then smashed the celebration champagne bottle across the ship's bow. To everyone's surprise, the bottle didn't break. Elizabeth tried a second time, and again the bottle stayed intact. Thankfully, the third attempt was successful.

But the rest of the launch was even more awkward than

The awkward side launch of the Edmund Fitzgerald *on June 8, 1958, and the heart attack death of an onlooker, led the superstitious to foresee a dark future for the vessel. (Photo from the author's collection.)*

the christening. Despite the herculean efforts of the shipyard crews, loosening the stubborn keel blocks underneath the vessel took more time than anticipated. Finally, after a delay of 36 minutes, eight electronically controlled guillotines dropped their razor-sharp blades to cut the hawsers (large ropes or cables) that were holding the ship. The *Edmund Fitzgerald* then slid thunderously down the 60 feet of wood timbers (smeared with train oil) and into the Detroit River. She entered the water sideways, crashing violently into the dock as her top half rolled to port, back to starboard, and then back to port again before stabilizing.

The side launch caused a huge wave to roll into the stands, soaking the stunned crowd. One onlooker, 58-year-old Jennings Frazier of Toledo, suffered a heart attack and died on the spot — the first casualty of the *Edmund Fitzgerald*. Superstitious sailors saw the death as an omen of bad luck for the vessel.

But the ship's namesake continued on with the official ceremonies. Addressing the audience at a celebration luncheon following the launch, Edmund Fitzgerald described how his grandfather and great uncles had left home to sail ships as soon as they had been old enough. He went on to say, "My boyhood ambition was to be a shipbuilder. My father was killed when I was six and our generation drifted away from the lake business, but we never ceased to love it and to have the desire to be a part of it. We see this ship as accomplishing just that."

The First Season

For the *Edmund Fitzgerald's* first season, the commissioning of the ship was given to Captain Bert Lambert, a veteran mariner who was close to retirement. On September 13, 1958, Lambert took the vessel down the Detroit River for sea trials on Lake Erie. Nine days later, on Monday, September 22, she was officially handed over to NMLIC for long-term charter to and operation by the Columbia Transportation Division of Oglebay Norton Company. At seven o'clock that morning, the *Edmund Fitzgerald*, under the command of Captain Lambert, headed north and officially began her Great Lakes shipping career.

The ship's first working voyage took her through Michigan's Sault Ste. Marie locks and into Lake Superior, where she set course for Silver Bay, Minnesota, to load 25,000 tons of taconite pellets. As the *Fitzgerald* sailed west across Lake Superior, she ran into strong headwinds — not unusual for that time of year. Then, sometime after midnight, the electronic control center in the engine room sparked and caught fire. Crewmembers Carl Makinen and Ed Chaput quickly headed to the standby generator to crank it up manually, but it wouldn't respond. The

"Fitzgerald" Named Ships

E. Fitzgerald, Schooner, 8790
- built in 1870 at Port Huron, Michigan by Fitzgerald & Leighton and named for Edmond Fitzgerald
- two masts at 297.84 tons
- wrecked at Long Point, Lake Erie during storm on November 14, 1883, with loss of life

R. P. Fitzgerald, Steamer, 110745
- built in 1887 at cost of $130,000 at Detroit, Michigan by the Detroit Dry Dock Co. For R. P. Fitzgerald (l/3), Philip D. Armour (l/3) and Wiley M. Egan (l/3); part of the "White Fleet"
- named for Robert Patrick Fitzgerald
- 1681.91 gross tons
- listed as abandoned in *Merchant Vessels* 1924 (reported that her timbers lie at bottom of Pine River, Michigan)

W. E. Fitzgerald, Steamer, 203561
- built as a bulk freighter in 1906 by Detroit Shipbuilding Co. for the Chicago Navigation Co.
- named in honour of William E. Fitzgerald of Milwaukee
- steel hull, 440 ft overall, 420 ft keel, 52 ft beam, 28 ft deep
- 1928, converted to a self-unloader
- home port Duluth, Minnesota when owned and operated by the Chicago Navigation Company from 1906 to 1930; sold in 1931 to Gartland Steamship Company of Delaware; home port changed to Chicago, then Wilmington, Delaware
- scrapped at Humberstone, Ontario during winter of 1971-72

Edmund Fitzgerald, Bulk Carrier, 277437
- built in 1958 at River Rouge, Michigan by the Great Lakes Engineering Works for the Northwestern Mutual Life Insurance Co. (NMLIC), Milwaukee
- named for NMLIC's Chairman of Board of Directors and President, Edmund Fitzgerald
- operated by Columbia Transportation Div., Oglebay Norton & Co., Cleveland
- sank in Lake Superior during storm November 10, 1975, with 29 lives lost

The 640-foot bulk freighter Carl D. Bradley, launched in 1927. (C. Patrick Labadie Collection, Lake Superior Maritime Collections, UW-Superior)

lighting system shut down next, and the ship drifted aimlessly in the dark. A few minutes later, the problem was fixed and the power came back on — but the incident lasted long enough to give everyone on board that eerie Titanic feeling.

On her return trip through the Soo Locks, the *Fitzgerald* broke the record for carrying the largest load of ore ever to pass through the locks. By the end of her two-month inaugural shipping season, she'd made 15 trips and carried about half a million tons of ore. (Although the ship was built to sail 45 to 50 trips a year, with each trip averaging five days, her inaugural season was short because her launch was late in the shipping year.)

The *Fitzgerald* finished her first season with a trip from Minnesota to Toledo, Ohio, on November 18, 1958. While still out on Lake Superior, Captain Lambert was warned about an impending storm. When the ship entered northern Lake Huron, she was met with gale-force winds reaching 70 knots.

As crewmember Edward Chaput later described, "All of the ship personnel not required below deck stayed topside for the day. Grown men were scared. The balance of the trip that late November day was under heavy winds and near 25-foot seas."

Also sailing in that November storm was the 640-foot bulk freighter *Carl D. Bradley*, one of the largest ships on the Great Lakes (the largest when launched in 1927). It was the *Bradley's* final voyage of the 1958 shipping year, and she was heading to dry-dock for $800,000 worth of overdue repairs. Earlier that season, the Coast Guard had certified the *Bradley* as seaworthy, even though the ship's crew and captain had voiced concerns about the condition of her hull. To their relief, the ship had held out, and everyone on board was glad that the season was almost behind them.

On November 17, the crew of the *Bradley* unloaded the ship's last cargo of limestone in Gary, Indiana, put 9000 tons of water in her ballast for stability, and, at 6:30 p.m., headed out on choppy Lake Michigan for the 30-hour trip to Calcite, Michigan.

The next day, the weather turned nasty. Gale warnings were posted and several ships on the lake headed to safe harbor to wait out the storm. But bad weather didn't stop large freighters like the *Bradley* — they were built to handle rough waters. The *Bradley's* captain, Roland Bryan, radioed ahead at 5:15 p.m. to say he expected his ship to arrive in Calcite at around 2 a.m.

The weather worsened. Winds increased to 57 knots, and the waves reached 20 to 30 feet. The *Bradley* flexed, twisted, and stressed her hull as she battled the high winds and heavy seas. At 5:30 p.m., when the ship was only 12 miles southwest of Gull Island in northern Lake Michigan, a sudden thud, followed by a vibration, shuddered through her. In the wheelhouse, Captain Bryan and First Mate Elmer Fleming looked back at the spar deck and saw the aft section sagging down. Both men knew immediately that the *Bradley* was starting to break apart.

Suddenly, a second thud pounded through the ship, and the stern sagged further. Fleming shouted "Mayday! Mayday! Mayday!" into the radio and then gave the *Bradley's* position, adding that they were in serious trouble. The distress signals were heard by both the Coast Guard and the German cargo motor vessel *Christian Sartori*. At the same time, over the intercom system, Captain Bryan ordered the crew to grab life jackets. Coast Guard members listened in shock as Fleming reported, "We're breaking up. We're going to sink. We're going down." Then Captain Bryan gave the signal to abandon ship: seven short blasts on the ship's whistle, followed by one prolonged blast.

Another thud trembled through the *Bradley*. The vessel sagged even more and then split in two near the No.10 hatch, approximately mid-ship. Power cables began to sever, and the lights and radio went dead. The ship's forward section rolled over and sank, and the life raft that was stowed forward floated free. As the crew tried to get off the ship, they were flung into the lake's frigid, churning waters. Before long, the *Bradley's* stern had plunged under the icy surface, throwing up flames and smoke as her boilers exploded. While Fleming and three of the crew made it onto a life raft, Captain Bryan stayed in the wheelhouse and went down with his ship.

Meanwhile, the *Christian Sartori*, commanded by former U-boat officer Captain Paul Mueller, was racing to the disaster scene. Mueller and his crew had seen the flash of flame and assumed the *Bradley* had exploded. Although the *Sartori* was only four miles away from the sinking ship, it took her almost two hours to reach the scene due to the rough seas.

By 11 p.m., two other vessels had joined the *Sartori* crew in their search for survivors. Overhead, planes dropped flares to light the search area, but it was almost impossible to spot a man or lifeboat in the black, stormy waters. Unknown to the rescuers, the four surviving crew members of the *Bradley* were firing flares of their own from the survival kit on the life raft. The men saved their last flare for signalling a rescue ship, but when one finally approached them, the flare failed to fire and the ship sailed by.

It was a horrible night for the survivors. Waves continuously swamped their life raft, and the men had to struggle to get back on the raft after being pitched into the water. Only two crew members survived the night — First Mate Fleming and 26-year-old watchman Frank Mays. By the time they were rescued by the U.S. Coast Guard cutter *Sundew* on the morning of November 19, the two men had drifted 20 miles from where the *Bradley* had gone down. They had been fighting to stay alive in the stormy seas for 14 hours.

In all, 33 crew members perished in the wreck of the *Bradley*, including Captain Bryan. Only 18 bodies were ever recovered, and each of them was wearing an approved cork life jacket, as were the two survivors. The Coast Guard investigation later concluded that one of the factors likely contributing to the vessel's break-up was an undetected structural weakness or defect.

The *Bradley* sank only 100 miles west of where the *Fitzgerald* had been sailing that same night, but the *Fitzgerald* crew didn't learn of the tragedy until they reached Toledo. A member of the crew later recalled the group's reaction to the news: "With great bravado and confidence born of hindsight, we all agreed that we were grateful to have sailed on the *Fitzgerald* instead."

Taking Care of Business

During her next few shipping seasons, the *Edmund Fitzgerald* broke several more records under her new captain, Newman C. "Joe" Larsen. In the summer of 1960, she surpassed her own tonnage record twice in two months: in July with a 25,828-ton load, and then in August with an even more impressive 26,451 tons. Later, in 1964, she became the first Great Lakes carrier

The 586-foot freighter Daniel J. Morrell, *sank in a November, 1966 storm. (C. Patrick Labadie Collection, Lake Superior Maritime Collections, UW-Superior)*

to haul a season total of more than 1 million tons of taconite through the locks at Sault Ste. Marie. The Great Lakes maritime community affectionately called her "Big Fitz."

Larsen retired after the 1965 season. The following year, command of the *Fitzgerald* went to Captain Peter P. Pulcher, a flamboyant, cigar-smoking shipmaster with 34 years' experience and a quirky sense of humour. Pulcher liked to have fun with his ship. Once, while taking the *Fitzgerald* through the Sault Ste. Marie Locks, he turned up the volume on his public address system and, in his booming voice, provided a commentary on the passage. On other occasions, when the *Fitzgerald* was sailing leisurely down the Detroit River, Pulcher would pipe the music of Mozart or Handel from the freighter's speakers, creating a bizarre scene for bystanders onshore.

Pulcher enjoyed the lighter side of life, but, as an experienced sailor and master, he had faced many dangerous situations and sailed through all kinds of bad weather. During his first year of command on the *Fitzgerald*, another treacherous storm on the Great Lakes took a deadly toll on fellow mariners.

It was the end of November 1966, and the 60-year-old, 586-foot freighter *Daniel J. Morrell*, commanded by Captain Arthur Crawley, had officially ended her shipping season but was making an unexpected extra trip to pick up a shipment originally meant for a vessel that had required immediate repairs. The *Morrell* was travelling in ballast (carrying no cargo) from Buffalo, New York, to Taconite Harbor, Minnesota, when an angry storm blew in. Suddenly, icy waves on Lake Huron reached 20 to 25 feet, winds blew at 35 to 40 knots with gusts to 57 knots, and visibility was reduced to about 4 miles. At around 12:15 a.m. on November 29, Captain Crawley radioed Captain Thomas Connelly on the nearby *Edward Y. Townsend* and informed him that the *Morrell* had been blown off course. The storm intensified and, just like the *Bradley* had done eight years earlier, the *Morrell* broke in half.

As the *Morrell* sank, her crew members, including Captain Crawley, positioned themselves on a pontoon life-raft on deck and waited for the bow section of the ship to slip out from under them. But while they waited, a huge wave came upon them and swept everyone into the frigid waters. Fighting wave after violent wave, four sailors managed to get back onto the raft. For nearly two days, they were viciously tossed around in the cold, heaving lake. It wasn't until 4 p.m. on November 30 that a Coast Guard helicopter sighted the life raft.

To the rescuers' dismay, it appeared that the raft held nothing more than four dead bodies. But as the helicopter hovered above the raft, the aircrew was suddenly shocked to see a hand and head pop up from among the heap. Watchman Dennis Hale had managed to stay alive by crawling under the corpses of his dead crewmates and using their still-warm bodies as protection against the elements. When he was finally taken off the raft, the half-naked Hale was semi-conscious and suffering from exposure, frostbite, a broken ankle, and other minor injuries. He claimed he owed his life to an apparition that had visited him on the raft and offered him survival tips, including the recommendation that he avoid eating ice chips because they would lower his body temperature. Hale was the only survivor from the *Morrell*; the other 28 crew members died.

The same night the *Morrell* went down, another terrible

shipwreck tragedy was narrowly averted after the storm-battered freighter *Edward Y. Townsend* — the last ship in contact with the *Morrell* — almost broke in two. Unknown to the *Townsend's* captain and crew, an 18-inch crack had opened up on her deck while she struggled in the storm. When she finally reached Sault Ste. Marie and the break was discovered, the U.S. Coast Guard immediately withdrew her certificate. (The ill-fated *Townsend* was never repaired. Two years later, in early October 1968, she broke in two and sank while being towed across the Atlantic Ocean to Spanish shipbreakers.)

Danger always shadowed the ships sailing the Great Lakes. Although captains and crews respected the destructive power of nature, they could not afford to let this power hold them back. Their ships were in the business of moving cargo quickly over the water — and if possible, breaking some shipping records along the way.

Under Pulcher's command, the *Fitzgerald* continued to break records. In June 1966, she became the first ship through the Soo Locks to transport a cargo exceeding 29,000 tons. Then in July 1967, she set a record that her crew had been seeking for a long time: 30,000 tons in a single trip. And in 1969, she carried more than 1.3 million tons of cargo through the Soo Locks in one season, setting yet another tonnage record.

It was also under Pulcher that the *Fitzgerald* underwent some major changes. In 1969, a diesel-powered bow thruster was installed in the ship to give her better maneuverability. Two years later, during the 1971–72 winter lay-up, she was converted from a coal-driven steamer to one that used oil-fired boilers.

During the Pulcher years, she also had a few collisions that resulted in damage to her hull. In 1969, for example, she ran aground while approaching the Soo Locks, harming her bottom and internal structure. The next year, she sustained damage above her waterline when she collided with the freighter Hochelaga. Then, later that season, she hit the wall of the Soo Locks again (she'd hit it twice before).

Pulcher retired at the start of the 1972 shipping season, and command of the *Edmund Fitzgerald* went to Captain Ernest Michael McSorley, a 59-year-old mariner with over 41 years of Great Lakes sailing experience. Of Irish heritage, McSorley was born in 1913 in Ogdensburg, New York. He began his career on the lakes at age 18, signing on as a deck hand and steadily moving up the ladder of command.

In 1951, just before his 38th birthday, McSorley became the youngest master on the Great Lakes when he took command of his first ship, the 255-foot *Carrolton*. For the next 21 years, the dark-haired, distinguished looking captain commanded eight other vessels — the *William E. Stifel*, the *Ben E. Tate*, the *Harry T. Ewing*, the *Robert J. Paisely*, the *J. B. Sensibar*, the *W. W. Holloway*, the *Joseph H. Franz*, and the *Armco*. Those who worked with McSorley learned quickly that he didn't socialize much with his crew; he preferred to maintain a professional, businesslike relationship with them. But his men respected and trusted him, and they had every confidence in his competence and skill.

On Sunday, November 9, 1975, Captain McSorley sailed the *Fitzgerald* out of Superior, Wisconsin, and into Lake Superior. The ship was loaded with taconite for the steel mills in Detroit. Since her launch in 1958, she had logged a total of 748 voyages and sailed over a million miles of water. This was to be her 17th year battling against the November storms on the Great Lakes.

II

Lake Superior:
The Spirit Ocean

The Great Lakes are the world's largest group of fresh-water lakes, containing nearly 20 percent of the earth's fresh surface water. Made up of Lake Superior, Michigan, Huron, Erie, and Ontario, the Great Lakes connect the middle of North America with the Atlantic Ocean and share borders with the Canadian province of Ontario and eight states: Minnesota, Wisconsin, Michigan, Illinois, Indiana, Ohio, Pennsylvania, and New York. Together, the five Great Lakes, and the channels that connect them, form a vital shipping system that has greatly shaped the industrial development of the United States and central Canada.

The largest of the Great Lakes, by far, is Lake Superior. Sometimes called the eighth sea, Lake Superior has the largest surface area of any lake in the world — about 31,700 square miles. With an average depth of 483 feet, Superior is 1332 feet at its deepest. Though the average underwater visibility of the lake is 27 feet, there are places where one can look down clear and deep to 100 feet.

Lake Superior contains so much water — 3 quadrillion

gallons — that it could fill all the other Great Lakes, plus three more Lake Eries. In fact, if the lake were spread over North and South America, the two continents would be under a foot of water. As Dr. Carl Richards, former director of the University of Minnesota Sea Grant Program, writes in *Superior Science*, "We're dealing with 10 percent of the Earth's fresh water. That's an incredible volume of water resting in the middle of a forest, in the middle of a continent, on top of a mixture of rock and sand. It's challenging to know how to begin describing it."

When early French explorers first came upon the massive lake, they called it *le lac superieur*, or "the upper lake," because it was located north of the other Great Lakes. But Lake Superior has been given other names, too. In the 1600s, Jesuit Claude Jean Allouez called it Lac Tracy in honour of a Quebec nobleman and official, but the name never stuck. The Ojibwa called the lake Kitche Gammi (or Gichigami), meaning "the great lake" or "big water." Henry Wadsworth Longfellow recorded this name as Gitchee Gumee in his 1855 epic poem, *The Song of Hiawatha*. Centuries earlier, the Anishinabe on the lake's northeastern shore knew Lake Superior as Chegaming, or "The Spirit Ocean."

Whatever name it is known by, Lake Superior is a breathtaking body of water. It is also one of the world's most dangerous for sailors. "Lake Superior is a little different than the other lakes," explains Great Lakes Captain Erik Wood. "When winds are calm, the views from just about any position on the ship are wonderful. It is very beautiful ... Some of my best memories are of barbeques on the fantail in almost perfect weather, little wind, bright sunshine, beautiful views and the companionship that goes along with being a sailor on the lakes."

But when Lake Superior is wild, she wreaks mayhem and terror. Many a captain has stood in his ship's pilothouse and watched as heaving waves, whipped up by a massive storm, have battered his vessel from all sides. Looking out the rear windows, these same captains have seen their ships' spar decks twist and turn. Each has heard his vessel groan loudly under the deafening, non-stop assault of wind and water. And each has listened in alarm to the crashing sounds inside his ship as she responds to the raging waves, lurching from one side to the other and causing loose objects to smash to the floor.

The weather on Lake Superior can stir up seas that are deadlier than those of stormy ocean waters. In minutes, powerful gale-force winds can bring a chaotic mix of waves, sleet, and snow. Reverend George Grant understood the lake's power after witnessing it first-hand during his 1872 cross-country expedition with Sir Sandford Fleming. Grant wrote: "Those who have never seen Superior get an inadequate, even inaccurate idea, by hearing of it spoken of as a 'lake' and to those who have sailed over its vast extent the word sounds positively ludicrous. Though its waters are fresh and clear, Superior is a sea. It breeds storms and rains and fogs, like the sea. It is as cold in mid-summer as the Atlantic. It is wild, masterful, and dread as the Black Sea."

The Graveyard of Ships

Lake Superior's most treacherous area is an 80-mile stretch along its southeastern edge, beginning at the Pictured Rocks (in Munising, Michigan) and ending at Whitefish Point.

Nicknamed "Shipwreck Coast" and "Graveyard of Ships" because of the dangerous shoals in the area, this heavily travelled region is the site of more than half of Lake Superior's 550 known major shipwrecks. Every ship that enters or leaves Lake Superior must pass Shipwreck Coast. Downbound ships heading out of Lake Superior sail by the area on their approach to the Soo Locks on the St. Mary's River — the only water connection between Lake Superior and Lake Huron. Likewise, upbound ships coming from Lake Huron must pass through the locks and sail by Shipwreck Coast to reach their ports of destination.

The first recorded shipwreck on Lake Superior took place just off Whitefish Point in 1816, when the North West Company's 64-foot vessel *Invincible* sank during a violent storm. At that time, no lighthouse existed at Whitefish Point. It wasn't until 1849 that a light was erected there. Twelve years later, in 1861, the original structure was replaced with a new one, by order of President Abraham Lincoln. Knowing that the American Civil War was imminent, the president had wanted a brighter lighthouse at Whitefish Point in order to provide safer passage to ships carrying war materials. The 80-foot iron pile tower built there that year still stands today, and its light, which has shone almost without fail, has been a crucial guidepost to ships struggling in frightening storm conditions.

Lake Superior is unpredictable at any time during the shipping season; it is plagued by thick fog in spring and freak storms in summer. But the most dangerous period of the shipping season is just before the freeze-up in late autumn, as this is when the worst storms blow in. During these storms, sailors and ships must battle brutal winds, enormous waves, blinding snow, and heavy fog. Coupled with these terrible conditions are such obstacles as ice floes, raft ice, and floating slush, all of which can cause extensive damage to defenseless vessels.

Icy rain has also caused trouble during late-autumn storms, coating hapless ships and wreaking severe havoc on board. Captain John Gilbert, former senior marine safety inspector with Transport Canada in Thunder Bay, Ontario, explains how a Great Lakes vessel can become covered in ice: "When the water temperature is close to freezing and the air temperature is a bit below freezing, any spray hitting the upper structures of the ship may freeze-up quickly, much like wax building up on dipped candles, in layers."

The ice starts as a thin, clear layer, then accumulates as the spray continues to splash on the ship's cold metal. "I have seen one-inch pipe handrails covered with a layer of ice eight or more inches in diameter," says Gilbert.

Major problems arise as the ice build-up thickens. Sailors tell stories of crews having to swing axes and sledgehammers to knock ice off their ships. In some instances, ice has cemented shut cabin doors and hatches. Small ships have been rolled over because of the tons of added weight. Indeed, the shimmering fairytale appearance of an ice-coated ship belies its dangerous condition.

But to many, the threat of ice coatings, ice floes, and thick slush is much less sinister than the threat of the Three Sisters. According to Superior lore, the "Three Sisters" are a rogue trio of huge waves that race along stormy waters, ramming anything in their path. The first wave in the trio slams onto a ship's deck. Then, before the backwash from this wave can clear away, the second wave — larger than the first — smashes mercilessly down on the beleaguered vessel. As the vessel struggles to recover from the powerful double-whammy, the last of the trio — and the largest of all — delivers the final, devastating hit, loading tons of water onto the ship and pushing her so deep underwater that sometimes she cannot power back up.

Are these Three Sisters simply folklore? A mariner's hyperbole? Sailors who have survived the deadly trio insist that the killer waves are real, and that they appear without warning on Lake Superior.

The Spirits of the Lake

Over the centuries, many have come to believe that a mystical sea monster is behind the violent conditions that bring disaster to those who sail Lake Superior. According to native legends, Superior's wild waters are controlled by a great sea creature called Mishipizheu (spelled various ways). In some of these tales, the evil and fearsome Mishipizheu is two beings — a horned serpent and an underwater lion. In others, Mishipizheu can change its appearance, taking on whatever form it desires.

In 1667, French missionary and explorer Claude Jean Allouez wrote that Native people brought calm to Lake Superior's wild waters by sacrificing sturgeon to the undersea monster. Two hundred years later, Bishop Frederick Baraga of Slovenia (famous as the "Snowshoe Priest" of Michigan's Upper Peninsula) referred to the creature as a "lion," while

Nicholas Perrot, a well-known 19th century French fur trader in Wisconsin, claimed it had a "large tail ... when he wiggles it lively it causes great tempests."

Close encounters with the creature were often so traumatic that, even years later, the most toughened men were still haunted by what they'd seen. Venant St. Germain was one such man. A reputable fur trader, voyageur, and shareholder with the North West Company, he began trading at Grand Portage in 1771 and had paddled his canoe across Lake Superior many times. On November 13, 1812, he went before the Court of King's Bench in the District of Montreal to swear that 30 years earlier, he, along with three other voyageurs and an elderly Ojibwa woman, had seen a "merman" near Pie Island (close to present-day Thunder Bay, Canada). The group had been travelling from Grand Portage to Mackinac and had made camp for the night at the south end of Pie Island when St. Germain spotted a half-human creature swimming nearby. The creature, he said, was the size of a seven- or eight-year-old child, with bright eyes, a small nose, and a brownish complexion. As St. Germain and the others stared at the merman, the curious but cautious creature stared back, but disappeared when there was a noisy confrontation on shore.

According to St. Germain, when he took out his rifle to shoot the creature, the Ojibwa woman grabbed him angrily, stopping him from firing a shot. She told him that the merman was the God of the Waters and Lakes, and then she predicted that because of St. Germain's violent intentions, the whole group would soon die in a vicious storm. At about 10 p.m. that night, the weather turned ugly and, for the next three days, wind and rain furiously battered the stranded foursome. Though the group survived the terrifying ordeal, its memory stayed with St. Germain for the rest of his life. Early Native peoples and fur traders weren't the only ones to see mysterious creatures in Lake Superior. On occasion, others, including lake captain George Robarge, claimed to have seen something around the dangerous entrance to Whitefish Point. On July 31, 1895, the Detroit Free Press reported: "Captain George Robarge, master of the propellor *S.S. Curry* says the sea serpent is not a myth. With his own eyes, he beheld the hideous monster. It was sunset, says the captain, on his last trip down from Duluth, when near White Fish Point (Lake Superior) that the antediluvian reptile thrust its long neck above the surface some 400 yards distant from the *Curry*. For fully five minutes, the submarine beast kept itself in view and amused itself by racing with the propellor."

Captain Robarge, along with his second mate and watchman, observed the creature through binoculars with great interest. As the newspaper article relayed: "The serpent's neck was some 15 feet in length and its jaws parted a foot or more. Ever and anon its body rose above the waters and revealed a strange undulating motion. Suddenly it disappeared and was seen no more."

According to native legend, Mishipizheu can be in different places at the same time and is often spotted during sudden squalls on Lake Superior. Legend also maintains that the monstrous waves that appear during a fierce storm are really Mishipizheu, combing the waters in search of new victims.

Veteran mariners, however, have often claimed that the ferocious late-autumn storms on the lake are actually the work of an entirely different entity: the Witch of November. It is her deadly concoctions, they say, that turn the lake's surface into a black cauldron of bone-chilling rain, drizzly sleet, hard snow, and brutal winds. And whenever the dark witch makes one of her potent brews, there are no safe spots for ships on the waters of Lake Superior.

The Witch's Brew

The Witch of November was hard at work November 28–30, 1905, when a destructive storm hit all five of the Great Lakes, sinking or stranding 16 ships. On Lake Superior, the temperature dipped to 12 degrees below zero within minutes, and hurricane-force winds churned the furious seas. Blinding snow and heavy waves pummelled the ships on the lake, but not all the chilling drama took place out on the open water.

In Duluth, Minnesota, more than 10,000 people lit bonfires and watched from shore as the 430-foot steamer *Mataafa* battled the storm. As the Duluth *Evening Herald* reported, "It seemed as though half the population of Duluth was on the pier's approach and along the shore watching the giant freighter going to her doom."

The *Mataafa* had departed Duluth earlier but, because of the storm, had decided to return. The drama began when the *Mataafa* tried unsuccessfully to re-enter the narrow channel of the Duluth Ship Canal, crashing her bow into the north pier's concrete wall. She was then pushed by violent winds into Lake Superior, settling in the water 100 feet from the pier and 700 feet from shore.

A three-day storm in November 1905 sent the 430-foot steamer Mataafa *to the lake bottom just 700 feet from the Duluth, MN shoreline and a huge crowd of onlookers. (Kennneth E. Thro Collection, Lake Superior Marine Museum Archive, UW-Superior)*

The waves were so rough that rescue of the *Mataafa* crew by lifeboat was impossible. Four attempts at a "breeches buoy" (shooting a line to the ship so the crew could ride it across the water to safety) also failed. The Duluth *Evening Herald* reported that the crowd "gasped" and "groaned" as wave after wave pounded the *Mataafa*, and that the ship itself seemed to be suffering greatly: "One would almost imagine the vessel had feelings of a human ... She shook and trembled under the terrific blows that were dealt her as though each caused excruciating pain."

The following day, Duluth's lifesaving crew finally reached the *Mataafa* and rescued 15 survivors. (Some reports say there were 16 survivors.) The lifesavers waited another day before returning to retrieve five men who were frozen on the ship's decks, having to cut them out of the ice. The bodies of four others, who had been swept overboard, were recovered later.

The 1905 storm was unquestionably wicked, but many consider a 1913 storm to be the worst ever on the Great Lakes.

Nicknamed the "Great Storm," or "White Hurricane," it began on Friday, November 7, with 78-knot winds, heavy snow, and thick fog. Sleet coated the vessels on the water, giving them an icy, opaque skin that sealed shut their doorways. Day and night, unrelenting, mountainous waves crashed over the ships, breaking windows and crushing cabins.

Particularly vulnerable were the vessels sailing on Lake Superior, including the 376-foot steel freighter *William Nottingham*. She had left Fort William, Canada (amalgamated with Port Arthur in 1970 to become present-day Thunder Bay) with a cargo of grain and was caught in the open lake at the height of the storm. For 48 hours, the *Nottingham* was tossed mercilessly in the freshwater sea, fighting to stay afloat. When the ship ran out of the coal needed to keep her boilers going, the desperate crew burned her furniture and wood trim. In no time, the wood was used up, and the crew members realized they would have to burn the ship's grain cargo for fuel.

Quickly, the hatches were opened and grain was shovelled onto the deck, then down the coal chutes into the bunkers, and finally into the engine room, where crew members furiously heaved wheat into the boilers. To everyone's relief, this kept the ship afloat as she desperately tried to reach the safe refuge of Whitefish Bay. As she drew near, the storm pushed the *Nottingham* ashore between Sand and Parisienne Islands, where she became wedged on the rocks.

Three crew members volunteered to take a lifeboat and get help, but as the lifeboat was being lowered into the stormy water, a wave slammed it — and the three men — against the ship. Moments later, the lifeboat rolled. The men fell into the icy waters and disappeared. The remaining crew members stayed on the *Nottingham* until they were rescued the next day.

At the other end of Lake Superior, the 249-foot Canadian bulk freighter *Leafield* was also overwhelmed by the storm. After leaving Port Arthur with a cargo of steel rails, she was driven onto the rocks near Angus Island, just 20 miles east of Thunder Bay. The waves and wind battered the *Leafield* continuously, pushing the ship and her 18 crew members into a cold, deep Superior grave.

By the time the Great Storm blew itself out on Monday, November 10, it had reportedly drowned more than 250 sailors on the Great Lakes, sunk a dozen ships, and pushed aground another 31 vessels.

It was 27 years before the Witch of November came back to claim more ships and crews. But when she did return, she did it in vicious style. On November 11, 1940, a storm system moved from the United States' Upper Midwest to Eau Claire, Wisconsin, then started its track over Lake Superior and the other Great Lakes.

And what a storm it was: hurricane-force winds, blinding blizzard conditions, and 35-foot waves. Known as the Armistice Day Storm of 1940, it wrecked a dozen vessels (two steel freighters sank without a trace) and killed 66 sailors. At least 162 people died on land and sea.

In the last 50+ years, a trio of large lake freighters have sunk during November storms: the *Carl D. Bradley* on November 18, 1958; the *Daniel J. Morrell* on November 29, 1966; and the *Edmund Fitzgerald* on November 10, 1975.

The 249-foot Leafield *fell victim to a 1913 Lake Superior storm, taking with it 18 crew members. (Photo from the author's collection.)*

Business, Not Bravado

It's not out of a sense of romanticism, bravado, or adventure that sailors dare to sail Lake Superior during the gales of November. Rather, they sail through the rough seas because it's their job to deliver as much cargo as their vessels can carry, and to do it quickly. From the steamers and sailing ships of the 19th century to the enormous freighters of today, most ships on the Great Lakes sail, or have sailed, for the same reason: to make money for ship owners and shipping companies. According to some, it was once common practice to reward captains with performance bonuses for exceeding company goals and/or making extra late-season trips.

The busiest shipping time on the Great Lakes — autumn — also happens to be the most dangerous period of the season. A lake freighter in good condition is designed to handle storm stresses, but occasionally, circumstances collide and "virtually unsinkable" super-ships go down.

The *Fitzgerald* was one such super-ship, even though she had lost her title as the largest Great Lakes freighter when the 838-foot *Roger Blough* was launched in 1971. And with the new era of mega-size lakers, like the U.S. Steel Company's 1000-foot freighter *Stewart Cort* launched in 1972, the *Fitzgerald's* record-making cargo loads were also a thing of the past.

Nevertheless, the *Fitzgerald* continued to be one of the biggest, most powerful vessels working on the Great Lakes. Her past feats and sustained reliability secured her reputation as a shipping icon — some even called her the "Pride of the American Flag."

No one could have imagined that she would soon gain worldwide fame as a tragic Great Lakes legend. But her end was near.

III

More than a Gale

The automobile industry was booming in 1975, and U.S. steel mills needed more taconite — lots more — to continue pumping out cars. Even as the shipping season was nearing its end on the Great Lakes, shipping companies were pushing many of their vessels to make a few more trips in order to carry extra loads to the steel mills.

The *Fitzgerald* was among these ships, but her busy season was threatened when her sailing license expired at the end of October. Not wanting to miss out on any extra profits to be made, the Oglebay Norton Company applied to the U.S. Coast Guard for a license extension. However, in order to get this extension, the ship needed to pass her annual spar deck inspection. In the previous 18 months, the *Fitzgerald* had already passed some other rigorous inspections by the Coast Guard, including a mandatory annual inspection in the spring of 1975 and an out-of-water inspection, which was required every five years.

On October 31, Lieutenant William R. Paul of Coast Guard Marine Safety carried out a spar deck inspection of the *Fitzgerald* in Toledo. He didn't like what he saw on the upper deck: 4 of the ship's 21 hatches failed to close properly

The Edmund Fitzgerald *departing Duluth-Superior harbor, 1975. (C. Patrick Labadie Collection, Lake Superior Maritime Collections, UW-Superior)*

due to cracks and gouges. Lieutenant Paul wrote to Oglebay Norton and informed the company that the *Fitzgerald* would not be allowed to sail the following year unless proper repairs were made. However, he considered the cracks and gouges to be routine seasonal damage and granted permission for the *Fitzgerald* to operate without the repairs for the rest of the 1975 shipping season.

One More Load

With the Coast Guard's approval to continue sailing, Captain McSorley and his crew prepared to squeeze in one last trip, maybe two, on the *Fitzgerald*. Before leaving Toledo, McSorley visited his wife, Nellie, who was living in a nearby nursing home while recovering from a stroke. Nellie's fragile health weighed heavily on McSorley's mind. He said goodbye to her, confident he would be spending more time with her once he retired at the end of the season. For now, though, he had to focus on taking the *Fitzgerald* to Superior, Wisconsin, to pick up yet another load of taconite.

By early Sunday morning, November 9, the *Fitzgerald* was docked in Superior at the Burlington Northern Railroad Dock 1. At 8:30 a.m., workers began loading the ship with the reddish-brown taconite pellets that were destined for the huge steel plant on Zug Island in the Detroit River. (For this trip, the *Fitzgerald* would be carrying 26,116 tons of iron ore.) While the workers continued with their task, the ship's first mate, 62-year-old John "Jack" Henkle McCarthy, watched the cargo carefully. As the chief mate, his responsibilities included supervising the loading and unloading of the *Fitzgerald*.

McCarthy was a veteran Great Lakes mariner. Born in Pittsburgh on July 14, 1913, he moved to Lakewood, Ohio, on the southern shore of Lake Erie, when he was 19 years old. A few years later, while working as a soda jerk in a drugstore in nearby Cleveland, he met A. E. R. Schneider, the marine director of Cleveland-Cliffs Inc., North America's largest producer of iron ore pellets. McCarthy asked Schneider to keep him in mind if any job opportunities opened up on one of the company's boats. The request paid off. In October 1935, Schneider contacted the 22-year-old McCarthy and told him to get down to the marina before 7 p.m. if he still wanted a job. By that evening, McCarthy had signed on with the Great Lakes carrier *Yosemite*.

A hard worker, McCarthy was awarded his Master's papers in the early 1940s, and he soon joined the Columbia Transportation Division of Oglebay Norton. While working on the *Sensibar*, he met Ernest McSorley, and the two men became close friends.

McCarthy was eventually made a Great Lakes captain, but his career as a commander was cut short in the summer of 1956, when he took a "wrong turn" with the self-unloader *Ben E. Tate*. McCarthy was sailing the *Tate* into Lake Erie when he put the ship on the rocks off Catawba Island, tearing out her bottom. Damage was estimated at $200,000, and McCarthy's career appeared to be over. However, after a Coast Guard hearing, he was back working on the lakes — but never again as a captain.

In 1970, McCarthy was transferred as first mate to the *Armco*, which, at that time, was under McSorley's command. Two years later, when McSorley became captain of the *Edmund Fitzgerald*, McCarthy agreed to join him as first mate. After three years of working on board the *Fitzgerald*, McCarthy, like his captain, was planning to retire at the end of the 1975 shipping season.

Now, as he stood in the ship's pilothouse and watched the workers load the taconite pellets, McCarthy kept a keen eye on the red, green, and white trim lights mounted on the stern deckhouse. If the white trim light was shining, it meant the ship was level. A green light meant the *Fitzgerald* was listing to starboard, and a red light meant she was listing to port. McCarthy adjusted the loading procedure whenever a red or green light appeared. It was crucial that the ship be loaded correctly so that when she sailed, she was level in the water.

After the cargo was loaded, McCarthy waited for the readings from the permanent Plimsol line markings on the ship's bow and stern. These "load line" marks show the deepest a ship can be loaded at any time. McCarthy used the readings to determine how deep the *Fitzgerald* was sitting in the water and whether she was in compliance with minimum freeboard regulations. (Freeboard is the distance from the deck to the waterline, or, in simpler terms, the amount of boat that is above the water.)

As established by the U.S. Coast Guard, a ship's exact minimum freeboard is greater in the winter than it is in the summer. In other words, a ship is required to load less cargo toward the end of a shipping season so that more of the vessel remains above the water. This lessens the chance of large storm waves reaching the ship's deck.

Originally, the *Fitzgerald* was designed and built to load to a freeboard of 14 feet, 3.5 inches in the winter. However, over the years, the Coast Guard gradually revised the freeboard requirements for the *Fitzgerald* and other ships so they could take on more cargo, putting them deeper in the water. By 1975, the *Fitzgerald's* minimum freeboard at the end of the shipping season was a mere 11 feet, 6 inches. This meant that in November of that year, the *Fitzgerald* was sitting almost three feet deeper in the water and carrying several hundred tons more cargo than she was built to handle. And she would be sailing with that deeper winter load during the most dangerous shipping time on Lake Superior.

As the *Fitzgerald* was still being loaded, a low pressure weather system — which Canadian and U.S. forecasters had first noticed over west Texas the previous evening — was moving northeast across Kansas, headed toward Michigan and Lake Superior. Winds were pushing a multi-layered cloud system into a circular motion, like a gigantic rotating wheel. But it was still clear and sunny on Lake Superior.

By 2:15 p.m., the loaded *Fitzgerald* was fueled up with 50,013 gallons of No. 6 fuel oil and ready to get out on the open water. As the ship backed away from the dock, the crew worked at securing her 21 hatch covers. Each cover was 54 feet long, over 11 feet wide, and weighed 14,000 pounds, and each had to be secured with 68 manually positioned Kestner clamps.

A slight breeze fluttered as the *Fitzgerald* passed the Superior breakwall at 2:52 p.m. and began her 40th voyage of the year. She accelerated to full speed as she entered the open waters of the lake.

There were 29 crew members on board the *Fitzgerald* this trip: a master (Captain McSorley), three licensed deck officers, a chief engineer, four licensed engineering officers, and 20 unlicensed personnel.

Along with Captain McSorley and First Mate McCarthy, the other officers were Second Mate James Pratt and Third Mate Michael "Big Mike" Armagost. Pratt was in charge of the ship's charts, technical publications, and compliance with government regulations, while "Big Mike" looked after safety, firefighting equipment, and emergency drills.

The ship's chief engineer was 60-year-old George John Holl, who had served in the U.S. Merchant Marine Corps during the Second World War. Holl considered the *Fitzgerald* to be the "ultimate engineering command."

Down in the galley, 62-year-old Robert Rafferty was the temporary steward in charge of the kitchen. He was responsi-

THE CREW OF THE S.S. EDMUND *Fitzgerald*
November 10, 1975

McSorley, Ernest Michael
Master
Toledo, Ohio

McCarthy, John "Jack" Henkle
First Mate
Bay Village, Ohio

Pratt, James A.
Second Mate
Lakewood, Ohio

Armagost, Michael Eugene
Third Mate
Iron River, Wisconsin

Holl, George John
Chief Engineer
Cabot, Pennsylvania

Bindon, Edward Francis
First Assistant Engineer
Fairport Harbor, Ohio

Edwards, Thomas Edgar
Second Assistant Engineer
Oregon, Ohio

Haskell, Russell George
Second Assistant Engineer
Millbury, Ohio

Champeau, Oliver Joseph
Third Assistant Engineer
Milwaukee, Wisconsin

Beetcher, Frederick J.
Porter
Superior, Wisconsin

Bentsen, Thomas D.
Oiler
St. Joseph, Minnesota

Borgeson, Thomas Dale
Able-Bodied Maintenance Man
Duluth, Minnesota

Church, Nolan Frank
Porter
Silver Bay, Minnesota

Cundy, Ransom Edward
Watchman
Superior, Wisconsin

Hudson, Bruce Lee
Deckhand
N. Olmsted, Ohio

Kalmon, Allen George
Second Cook
Washburn, Wisconsin

MacLellan, Gordon F.
Wiper
Clearwater, Florida

Mazes, Joseph William
Special Maintenance Man
Ashland, Wisconsin

O'Brien, Eugene William
Wheelsman
St. Paul, Minnesota &
Perrysburg, Ohio

Peckol, Karl Anthony *Watchman* *Ashtabula, Ohio*	Spengler, William J. *Watchman* *Toledo, Ohio*
Poviach, John Joseph *Wheelsman* *Bradenton, Florida*	Thomas, Mark Andrew *Deckhand* *Richmond Heights, Ohio*
Rafferty, Robert Charles *Temporary Steward (First Cook)* *Toledo, Ohio*	Walton, Ralph Grant *Oiler* *Fremont, Ohio*
Riippa, Paul M. *Deckhand* *Ashtabula, Ohio*	Weiss, David Elliot *Deck Cadet* *Agoura, California*
Simmons, John David *Wheelsman* *Ashland, Wisconsin*	Wilhelm, Blaine Howard *Oiler* *Moquah, Wisconsin*

ble for feeding four meals a day to the *Fitzgerald* crew. Rafferty had spent over 30 years working in the galleys of big ships but had only come on board the *Fitzgerald* the month before, filling in for the ship's ailing chief cook. On the job, Rafferty created his own recipes, preparing everything from delicious soups to fresh homemade breads. He talked of retiring at the end of the season and liked the idea of capping his long sailing career by working on the famous *Fitzgerald*.

There were two other men on board the *Fitzgerald* who were also planning to retire at the end of the 1975 shipping season: special maintenance man Joseph William "Jugsy" Mazes and watchman Ransom Edward Cundy. Another Great Lakes veteran, Mazes was a lifelong bachelor who loved to fish and spend time with his siblings, nieces, and nephews. His crewmate Cundy had become a Great Lakes sailor after serving in the U.S. Marine Corps during World War II. The father of two daughters, Cundy had been devastated the previous year when his elder daughter was murdered by her husband. Cundy was the only man on board the *Fitzgerald* who could not swim.

Other war veterans among the ship's crew included oiler Blaine Howard Wilhelm, a Great Laker for 19 years who had served with the U.S. Navy in World War II and the Korean War, and third assistant engineer Oliver Joseph "Buck" Champeau, a Korean War veteran who had served with the Marines on *USS Oriskinay.*

As the *Fitzgerald* steamed into open waters that afternoon, the storm system heading for Lake Superior gathered intensity. The National Weather Service (NWS) predicted that northeast winds on the lake would increase significantly and then shift to the northwest by the next afternoon. Captain McSorley was aware of impending conditions, but at that point the weather system appeared to be nothing more serious than a typical late-autumn gale.

Storm Warning

Just up the coast from Superior, Wisconsin, another ship was making her way into open waters. The 767-foot iron ore carrier *Arthur M. Anderson* of the United States Steel Corporation left Two Harbors, Minnesota, at around 3:30 p.m., loaded with taconite bound for a steel mill in Gary, Indiana. Named after the director of U.S. Steel, the *Anderson* was one of eight AAA class ships built in the early 1950s. At her helm for this voyage was

Captain Jesse "Bernie" Cooper, a stocky man with over 30 years experience on the Great Lakes. According to Cooper, when the *Anderson* departed Two Harbors that afternoon conditions had been ideal: "It was one of those really special days on Lake Superior. It was warm, ripples on the water. It was a beautiful clear November day."

But soon after the *Anderson* left Two Harbors, an updated NWS broadcast informed all Lake Superior mariners that they should expect sustained gale-force winds at 34 to 48 knots that night. Again, this was considered fairly typical for the time of year.

The *Anderson* was about 10 miles away from the *Fitzgerald*, travelling on a parallel track. Soon after the NWS broadcast, Captain Cooper radioed Captain McSorley. The two men discussed the weather advisory. Both had travelled the area hundreds of times in bad weather. They knew November storms could cause sudden chaos on the lake, but they were confident in their sailing abilities, gained from decades of marine experience. They knew how to push their ships through poor conditions, adjusting their route when necessary. As Cooper would later recall, "That evening it didn't look like anything that was really out of the ordinary, might be a fresh gale or something, nothing for these particular ships ..."

As the two monster freighters steamed northeast, the NWS continued to broadcast gale warnings for Lake Superior throughout the evening. The storm was intensifying, and the two captains could feel their ships groan and twist in response to the building waves.

By 1 a.m. on November 10, the *Fitzgerald* was 19.8 miles

south of Isle Royale's Siskiwit Bay and 37.9 miles west of Eagle Harbor on Michigan's Keweenaw Peninsula. Temperatures had fallen to 37 degrees Fahrenheit, winds were shrieking, and 10-foot waves buffeted the ship. The *Fitzgerald's* officer on watch radioed to the NWS to give the first of the ship's four daily weather reports. (The others were scheduled to occur at 7 a.m., 1 p.m., and 7 p.m.) The 1 a.m. report was as follows: "Winds from the northeast at 52 knots with an overcast sky and visibility two to five miles in continuous heavy rain."

The deadly brew in the witch's cauldron was simmering. Mishipizheu was thrashing. By 2 a.m., weather conditions had worsened dramatically. The NWS broadcast a special bulletin: the gale warning was upgraded to a storm warning, with winds from the northwest up to 50 knots expected for the following afternoon.

IV

Raging Seas

As the winds howled across Lake Superior, cold rain pounded down on the choppy seas, and sharp, angled waves pushed freezing spray onto the decks of the *Fitzgerald* and the *Anderson*.

Shortly after the 2 a.m. storm warning, Captain McSorley and Captain Cooper discussed the deteriorating weather conditions over radiotelephone. They decided to alter their course, departing from the regular downbound route along the southern shore of Lake Superior and instead following the longer northern track in order to take advantage of the lee provided by the Canadian shore. This safer route, which would lessen the storm's impact on their vessels, would take them northeastward — past Isle Royale, Thunder Bay, Black Bay, and Nipigon Bay — and then eastward along the lake's northern shore before turning southeastward along the eastern shore. The last part of the route would be an open water run past Michipicoten Island and Caribou Island, then on to Whitefish Bay and the Soo Locks.

During the first 10 or so hours of the voyage, the *Anderson* had been leading the way. However, sometime around 3 a.m. on November 10, when the ships passed Isle Royale, the *Fitzgerald*, which was the faster ship, passed the *Anderson*.

At 7 a.m., both vessels were still steaming northeast when they filed their routine weather reports with the NWS. Captain McSorley also contacted Oglebay Norton's head office in Cleveland and explained that the *Fitzgerald* would be arriving at the Soo Locks later than expected due to bad weather.

On the water, visibility ranged from one to five miles, and winds were blowing northeast at 30 to 50 knots. The center of the storm system was now on the southern shore of Lake Superior, over Marquette, Michigan. As the system headed northeast over the lake, it was on a track that would take it west of Michipicoten Island — and on a collision course with the *Fitzgerald* and *Anderson*. Along the way, it would scoop up the summer heat from the water, adding energy to its fury.

Sometime between 9 a.m. and 10 a.m. — when they were only about 25 miles from the lake's northern shoreline — the *Fitzgerald* and the *Anderson* changed to an eastward course, sailing parallel to Ontario's shoreline for lee, as planned. At 10:30 a.m., another revision to the weather forecast was issued for eastern Lake Superior. The NWS now predicted that winds would shift in the afternoon from north to northwest, blowing at 32 to 48 knots, and then become northwesterly at 25 to 48 knots in the night. Waves could reach anywhere from 8 to 16 feet in height.

Just before noon, the two ships turned to a southeast course in order to make the run to Whitefish Bay. The winds screamed and smashed the waves hard against the vessels as the storm system continued to make its way across Lake Superior.

Suddenly, just after noon, skies cleared and the winds became relatively calm near the surface of the lake. Though

The 767-foot iron ore carrier Arthur M. Anderson *sailed from Two Harbors, Minnesota on a track parallel to the ill-fated* Edmund Fitzgerald. *(Painting by Capt. C (Bud) Robinson.)*

the change in the weather may have been a welcome relief to less experienced mariners, the two captains knew better: they had entered the eye of the storm. Swirling around the 20-mile calmness of the eye were rotating walls of dense clouds, strong winds, hard rains, and heavy turbulence. The "perfect storm" was just beyond the calm of the eye.

When the two ships headed out of the eye and into the northeast side of the eye wall, they crossed into the most treacherous part of the storm. (Cooper later stated that it was essentially a hurricane.) As expected, the system was now moving in a counter-clockwise direction — the winds had shifted and were coming from the northwest.

The *Fitzgerald* was the first of the two ships to sail out of the eye, just past the west end of Michipicoten Island. As soon as she passed through the ominous storm walls, sailing conditions quickly deteriorated.

Meanwhile, the storm cut a swath of destruction all along the Great Lakes. On Lake Erie, it sank a commercial fishing boat, killing two crew members. It also caused severe erosion and destroyed many buildings along the lake's shore. On Lake Michigan, two youths drowned after being washed off a break-wall. And St. Mary's River overflowed its banks and flooded the main street of Sault Ste. Marie, Michigan.

Sailing Blind

By mid-afternoon on November 10, the *Fitzgerald* was about 16 miles ahead of the *Anderson* as she steamed southwest of Michipicoten Island. Captain McSorley advised the *Anderson* that his ship was "rolling some." He then steered the *Fitzgerald* into the 22-mile-long channel leading toward Caribou Island, a small, diamond-shaped piece of land about three miles inside the Canadian border.

Caribou Island sits on a thin bedrock ridge approximately nine miles long. Because of this ridge, the waters around the island are shallow and rocky, with shoals extending out in places for miles. Particularly dangerous are the Six Fathom Shoals, extending into Lake Superior north of the island. These shallow waters can turn wild during November storms, creating huge waves that are strong enough to lift a vessel and smack her down into the troughs. Big lakers laden with cargo are especially vulnerable to these waves, because they are already sitting deep in the water. As they are tossed around like toy ships, the freighters are at risk of touching down (shoaling) on the rocky bottom, ripping holes in their hulls and straining — even breaking — a ship's fence railings and cables. Worse still, a captain and crew might not even know that their ship has shoaled, as the deafening noise of a storm can often mask the sounds of the impact.

As the *Fitzgerald* and the *Anderson* pushed on toward Caribou Island, nature's unleashed fury attacked them relentlessly. Under ominous, grey skies, gale-force winds kicked up squalls of snow and sleet. Waves peaked at over 16 feet, sloshing dreaded green water (water that lands on a ship's deck, adding tons of weight) onto both ships.

Captain Cooper, concerned that the *Anderson* was going to get too close to Caribou Island, adjusted his ship's course slightly so she would pass about six miles north of the island. Then, from the pilothouse, he and his first mate, Morgan Clark, watched as the *Fitzgerald*, still sailing ahead of the *Anderson*, approached the area of the Six Fathom Shoals. Cooper remarked to Clark that the *Fitzgerald* was drifting too close to the area where, in places, the water was barely 36 feet deep.

Around 3:15 p.m., the *Fitzgerald* was still working her way through the treacherous waters around Caribou Island when, suddenly, the snow and sleet turned into a blinding snowstorm. Monster waves now washed over her deck and that of the *Anderson*, coating both ships in ghostly, opaque ice. Whiteout conditions brought visibility to zero. Cooper lost sight of the *Fitzgerald*, but continued to track her progress on radar.

At about 3:30 p.m., within 15 minutes of passing out of the shoals area, the *Fitzgerald* sent an ominous message to the *Anderson*:

FITZGERALD: Anderson, *this is the* Fitzgerald. *I have sustained topside damage. I have a fence rail down, two vents lost or damaged, and a list. I am checking down. Will you stay by me 'til I get to Whitefish?*

ANDERSON: Charlie on that Fitzgerald. Do you have your pumps going?

FITZGERALD: Yes, both of them.

The *Fitzgerald* was taking on water, causing her to list to the left, but she had plenty of pumping power to get the water out: four electric main pumps that could push out 7000 gallons of water a minute, and two auxiliary pumps that could push out 2000 gallons a minute.

With such pumping power, why had McSorley checked down (slowed) his ship's speed and asked Cooper to close the distance between the vessels? By slowing her speed, McSorley was putting the *Fitzgerald* at risk of being pushed by the waves into a trough and making it tougher for the ship to have enough power to pull out.

Nevertheless, checking down wasn't an unusual move given the circumstances of the storm, and it didn't raise any red flags to any crew members listening to the radio on other ships. But did McSorley sense there was something more serious happening to the *Fitzgerald* that he did not want to broadcast?

"He gave no indication that he was worried or that he had a problem or there was something that he couldn't cope with," Cooper later told the U.S. Coast Guard Board of Inquiry.

Of course, it was not unusual for Great Lakes captains to say very little to each other while sailing, even if they were worried about the possibility of sinking. Anything they said on the ship's radio could be heard by everyone on the lake. If a captain raised an alarm about the ship's condition and then made it safely to port, his reputation and career could be jeopardized.

Shortly after the *Fitzgerald* checked down, the weather worsened. The Coast Guard advised all ships to immediately seek safe harbor until the storm passed. Conditions had become so dangerous that hurricane-force gusts were recorded at the Soo Locks, prompting officials to close them.

But the *Fitzgerald* and the *Anderson* could not seek safe harbor — the freighters were in open water and had to keep going. By 4 p.m., the northwest wind gusts were pummelling the two ships as they forged ahead on their straight run to the refuge of Whitefish Bay.

Suddenly, Captain McSorley's voice was heard again on the *Anderson's* radio. He had more bad news.

FITZGERALD: Anderson, *this is the* Fitzgerald. *I have lost both radars. Can you provide me with radar plots 'til we reach Whitefish Bay?*

ANDERSON: *Charlie on that,* Fitzgerald. *We'll keep you advised of your position.*

The freighters continued on, with the *Anderson* plotting the way for the *Fitzgerald* as McSorley and his officers kept the ship ploughing through the murderous seas. Cooper later recalled, "We were running plots every half-hour and marked her position and ours on the chart."

By 4:30 that afternoon, darkness had begun to set in. The waves were now regularly reaching over 16 feet, with winds blowing around 58 knots. Aboard the *Anderson*, crew members fought down their fear. At one point, more than 12 feet of water flooded the deck, making the pilothouse and sternhouse seem like small islands in a sea of foam, snow, and heaving water.

Meanwhile, the only navigation aid that appeared to be still working on the *Fitzgerald* was the radio direction finder. With that, McSorley tried to get a light or radio beam from the automated Whitefish Point Light. He knew the lighthouse was ahead of him, somewhere, and he seemed frustrated when he couldn't reach the signals. Unknown to the crew of the *Fitzgerald*, winds had struck the lighthouse, knocking down power to both the light and the beacon.

With alarm clearly in his voice, McSorley put out a call for any vessel in the vicinity of Whitefish Point. Captain Cedric C. Woodward answered. A veteran mariner, Woodward was sailing upbound around Whitefish Point, hired on as the Great Lakes registered pilot for the Swedish-flagged saltwater vessel *Avafors*.

Woodward knew McSorley and had talked to him often, but on November 10, he did not recognize McSorley's voice at first — it sounded strained and strange. McSorley asked Woodward if the Whitefish Point beacon or light were on. Woodward replied that he could not see the light or receive the beacon.

Next, McSorley called the Coast Guard Station at Grand Marais, Michigan, to ask if the Whitefish Point radio beacon was operating. The Coast Guard checked, found there had been a power failure, and informed McSorley that the beacon was not operating.

With no radio signal available at Whitefish Point, and having already lost both of her radars, the ice-coated *Fitzgerald* was sailing blind in one of the worst storms ever to hit Lake

Swedish saltwater vessel Avafors, *exchanged radio communications with the struggling* Fitzgerald *in the growing darkness and worsening storm. (Photo from the author's collection.)*

Superior. She was now totally reliant on the *Anderson* to guide her the remaining 35 miles to Whitefish Bay. To make matters worse, the *Fitzgerald's* powerful pumps could not keep the water out of the ship, and she began to ride deeper in the water, listing to one side.

At approximately 5:45 p.m., Captain Woodward called the *Fitzgerald* to give McSorley some good news.

AVAFORS: Fitzgerald, *this is* Avafors. *I have the Whitefish light now, but am still receiving no beacon. Over.*

FITZGERALD: I'm very glad to hear it.

AVAFORS: The wind is really blowing down here. What are the conditions where you are?

Suddenly, in the middle of the conversation, McSorley was distracted by something he saw on deck from the pilothouse — something so catastrophic that, without turning off the radio's microphone, he yelled, "Don't let nobody on deck!" These words were followed by something unintelligible and then, "... vents."

AVAFORS: What's that, Fitzgerald? Unclear. Over.

FITZGERALD: I have a bad list, lost both radars, and am taking heavy seas over the deck. One of the worst seas I've ever been in.

Captain Woodward later recalled that sometime between his two conversations with McSorley, he had overheard the *Anderson* tell the *Fitzgerald* that she was about 20 miles from Whitefish Point and that the *Anderson* was about 10 miles behind her and gaining.

The Last Hour

At around 6:20 p.m., the *Anderson's* first mate, Morgan Clark, grew concerned that the *Fitzgerald* had gone off course. Radar showed that she was veering off to his left. Clark radioed McSorley, who reported he was on the same heading as the *Anderson*, which meant they should be on the same track. It then occurred to Clark that perhaps the *Fitzgerald* had a new problem: it was possible that her gyrocompass was not working properly.

Winds were steady at 60 knots, gusting to more than 100 miles per hour (Category 2 hurricane-force). It was an ugly sea, churning as if someone had turned on an invisible mixer at high speeds.

Captain Cooper and First Mate Clark were monitoring their radar closely when they felt an unexpected bump and the *Anderson* lurched. The men turned to look behind them and were startled to see a huge wave pouring green water over their entire vessel. Starting from the stern, the water continued to roll along the deck, crashing into the back of the pilothouse

35 feet above the waterline and then driving the bow of the *Anderson* down into the seas. Fighting the water, the crew got the bow back up, but the Witch of November was not giving up just yet. As Cooper recalled, "Another wave just like the first one or bigger hit us again."

The second wave put more green water on the bridge deck, and this time, the water stayed on the deck for a longer period. But, as frightening a scene as it was, Cooper had every confidence in his ship: "That old girl *Anderson*, she came out shaking like a dog shaking water off, water flying all over ... I never gave it a thought. We had a good ship under us."

Knowing that the rogue waves that had just slammed the *Anderson* would be racing toward the wounded *Fitzgerald*, Cooper couldn't help but feel concerned. Travelling about a mile a minute, the super waves would hit the *Fitzgerald* about 10 minutes later — either that, or they would miss her entirely. Whatever happened, Cooper knew that McSorley, like any veteran Great Lakes mariner, would handle the situation as best he could.

At 7:10 p.m., Cooper left the wheelhouse to get his pipe. While he was gone, Clark radioed the *Fitzgerald* to tell McSorley about a vessel moving out of Whitefish Bay.

ANDERSON: Fitzgerald, *this is the* Anderson. *Have you checked down?*

FITZGERALD: *Yes, we have.*

ANDERSON: Fitzgerald, *we are about 10 miles behind you, and gaining about 1 1/2 miles per hour.* Fitzgerald, *there is a target 19 miles ahead of us. So the target is nine miles ahead.*

FITZGERALD: Well, am I going to clear?

ANDERSON: Yes, he is going to pass to the west of you.

FITZGERALD: Well, fine.

Just as First Mate Clark was going to sign off, he added:

ANDERSON: Oh by the way, how are you making out with your problem?

FITZGERALD: We are holding our own.

ANDERSON: Okay, fine. I will be talking to you later.

Soon after this exchange, Captain Cooper returned to the pilothouse and Clark told him what McSorley had said. At that point, the *Fitzgerald* was about 14 miles away from the safety of Whitefish Bay — just a little over 90 minutes' sailing time.

Cooper looked at the *Anderson's* radar screen and saw that the high seas and snow squalls were distorting the radar signals. Because of the distortion, the center of the radarscope soon became a "white blob," and the radar blip that had been representing the *Fitzgerald* disappeared into it.

At around 7:25 p.m., the snow squall stopped and the radar screen cleared. The *Fitzgerald* blip, however, did not return to the screen. As Cooper later explained, "I called the *Fitzgerald* on the FM and I got no response. The mate tried to call him several times."

Like Cooper, Clark received no reply. Where was the *Fitzgerald*?

V

When the Snow Stopped

When the snow squall ended that evening, visibility improved enough for Cooper and his officers to see for miles. Fighting down their mounting concern, they searched for the *Fitzgerald's* lights. They were able to make out lights in the far distance, but these were 17 miles away and, it turned out, belonged to the three saltwater vessels leaving Whitefish Bay — the *Avafors*, the *Benfri*, and the *Nanfi*. The *Fitzgerald's* lights were nowhere to be seen, yet she had been only eight or nine miles away from the *Anderson* when she'd disappeared from radar.

First Mate Clark checked his radar screen again. "We had something around six and a half, seven miles. But it would hold, maybe two sweeps, and then it would disappear," he recalled.

Captain Cooper and his officers began to wonder if perhaps the *Fitzgerald* had suffered a power blackout. With their binoculars, they scoured the horizon looking for a ship's outline. The *Fitzgerald* had to be there.

Suddenly, the *Anderson's* third mate, Robert May, saw a white light. It was just to the right of a red one (later determined to be a tower at Coppermine Point, Ontario). When no one else could see the white light, May thought perhaps he had seen a "light flare," a Great Lakes phenomenon caused by straining the eye when trying to see something at night far away.

Seconds, then minutes, ticked by. In the pilothouse, Cooper and Clark continued calling the *Fitzgerald* on the radio. Silence came back in return. Cooper later wrote, "At this time, I became very concerned about the *Fitzgerald* — couldn't see his lights when we should have. I then called the *William Clay Ford* (a 647-foot freighter waiting out the storm in Whitefish Bay) to ask him if my phone was putting out a good signal and also if perhaps the *Fitzgerald* had rounded the point and was in shelter. After a negative report ... I was sure something had happened to the *Fitzgerald*."

At 7:39 p.m., about half an hour after the last transmission from McSorley, Cooper used the distress Channel 16 frequency to make his first call to the U.S. Coast Guard at Sault Ste. Marie, Michigan, regarding the *Fitzgerald*. He was told by the radioman to call back on Channel 12 (the Coast Guard was busy trying to locate a missing 16-foot open fishing boat and presumably wanted the distress line free). But when Cooper called back on this frequency, he couldn't get through.

"Do You Realize What the Conditions Are?"
It would be almost an hour later, at 8:32 p.m., before Cooper finally talked to radioman Philip Branch.

ANDERSON: This is the Anderson. *I am very concerned with the welfare of the steamer* Edmund Fitzgerald. *He was right in front of us, experiencing a little difficulty.*

He was taking on a small amount of water, and none of the upbound ships have passed him. I can see no lights as before, and I don't have him on radar. I just hope he didn't take a nose dive.

COAST GUARD: This is Soo Control. Roger. Thank you for the information. We will try and contact. Over.

Why didn't anyone, other than the crew of the *Anderson*, seem to be concerned that a large, seemingly invincible lake freighter had just disappeared during a violent storm on Lake Superior? Philip Branch at Soo Control did try contacting the *Fitzgerald* and also advised the Coast Guard's Rescue Coordination Center (RCC) that there was some uncertainty about the *Fitzgerald*. However, it wasn't until after Cooper's fourth call to Soo Control, at 9:03 p.m., that the RCC launched a search and rescue operation.

Immediately, the Coast Guard Air Station at Traverse City, Michigan, ordered search and rescue aircraft to be dispatched. At 9:16 p.m., the rescue center at Canadian Forces Base Trenton (CFBT) was advised. Then, at 9:25, the Coast Guard's nearby 110-foot harbor tug *Naugatuck* was directed to leave Sault Ste. Marie.

But there was a problem: the *Naugatuck* was restricted from operating outside of harbor waters when the wind was moving at more than 60 knots — and on the night of November 10, it was. So, while *Fitzgerald* crew members may have been struggling in the freezing waters of Lake Superior, the *Naugatuck*, only 17 miles away, was forced to stay put in Whitefish Bay. (When the winds finally did die down sufficiently, the *Naugatuck* was again delayed due to mechanical problems. She didn't arrive on the search scene until 12:45 the next afternoon — more than 15 hours after first being called out.)

The Coast Guard's only search and rescue (SAR) surface unit large enough to cope with severe weather and rough sea conditions was the *Woodrush*, a 180-foot buoy tender that was over 300 miles away in Duluth. Despite her faraway location, at 9:30 p.m. the *Woodrush* was ordered to make her way to the search site. Already on six-hour SAR standby readiness, she was underway within two and a half hours, making the 24-hour journey to the site.

At 10:06 p.m., the first rescue aircraft, a fixed-wing HU-16, left Traverse City headed for the last known position of the *Fitzgerald*, as given by the *Anderson*. Seventeen minutes later, a Sikorsky HH-52 helicopter equipped with Nightsun (an externally mounted xenon searchlight with 3.8 million candlepower) lifted off from the same airport. A short while later, a second helicopter took off.

By this point, more than three hours had passed since anyone had heard from the *Fitzgerald*. The *Anderson*, meanwhile, had reached the shelter of Whitefish Bay. The crew members were exhausted, but relieved to be out of the storm they had battled for over 36 hours. They were also just beginning to fully realize the tragic fate of their travelling companion, the *Fitzgerald*.

At the same time, officials were still trying to get a rescue vessel — any rescue vessel — to the *Fitzgerald* site in the coming hours. Desperate, the commanding officer of the Coast Guard in Sault Ste. Marie put in a call to Captain Cooper:

COAST GUARD: Anderson, this is Group Soo. What is your present position?

ANDERSON: We're down here, about two miles off Parisienne Island right now ... the wind is northwest 40 to 45 miles here in the bay.

COAST GUARD: Is it calming down at all, do you think?

ANDERSON: In the bay it is, but I heard a couple of the salties talking up there, and they wish they hadn't gone out.

COAST GUARD: Do you think there is a possibility that you could ... ah ... come about and go back there and do any searching?

Cooper paused.

ANDERSON: Ah ... God ... I don't know ... ah ... that ... that sea out there is tremendously large. Ah ... if you want me to, I can, but I'm not going to be making any time. I'll be lucky to make two to three miles an hour going back that way.

COAST GUARD: Well, you'll have to make a decision as to whether you will be hazarding your vessel or not, but you're probably one of the only vessels right now that can get to the scene. We're going to try to contact those saltwater vessels and see if they can't possibly come about and possibly come back also ... things look pretty bad right now; it looks like she may have split apart at the seams like the Morrell *did a few years back.*

ANDERSON: Well, that's what I been thinking.

COAST GUARD: Well, again, do you think you could come about and go back and have a look in the area?

ANDERSON: Well, I'll go back and take a look, but, God,

73

I'm afraid I'm going to take a hell of a beating out there ... I'll turn around and give 'er a whirl, but, God, I don't know. I'll give it a try.

COAST GUARD: That would be good if you could turn around and head out that way, and we'd like to get as many other vessels that can possibly get underway and proceed to that area.

ANDERSON: Do you realize what the conditions are out there?

The Coast Guard did not answer.

ANDERSON: You do realize what the conditions are out there, don't you?

COAST GUARD: Affirmative. From what your reports are I can appreciate the conditions. Again, though, I have to leave that decision up to you as to whether it would be hazarding your vessel or not. If you think you can safely go back up to that area, I would request that you do so. But I have to leave that decision up to you.

ANDERSON: I'll give it a try, but that's all I can do.

When the *Anderson's* chief engineer told the rest of the ship's crew that they were turning around and heading back out, one sailor was reported to have gone back to his room, recorded his last will and testament on a tape recorder, sealed it in wax, and placed it in a jar — just in case.

Soo Control also contacted the three upbound saltwater ships that were travelling slightly northwest of the *Fitzgerald's* search site and asked if they would go to the site. On the *Nanfri*, Captain Albert Jacovetti agreed to slow down his ship and slightly alter course to pass closer to the site, but he said it would be impossible to actually turn his ship around. The captain of the *Benfri* declined outright, as did the captain of the *Avafors* — neither was willing to hazard their ocean freighters and crew in such dangerous conditions.

In the safety of Whitefish Bay, there were at least seven ships anchored. The commanding officer of the Coast Guard radioed all of them: "Is there any way possible that you could get underway and search for the survivors?"

Only the *William Clay Ford*, commanded by Captain Don Erickson, and the Canadian 730-foot bulk carrier *Hilda Marjanne* answered the call to leave Whitefish Bay and join the search. Within 30 minutes, however, the monstrous seas proved to be too much for the *Hilda Marjanne*, and she was forced to return to the bay. This meant that, on the night of November 10, the primary search and rescue vessels were the storm-battered *Anderson* and the *William Clay Ford*.

Searching Through the Night

After 10 p.m., the media began to broadcast news of the missing *Edmund Fitzgerald* on radios and televisions across the world. Some people held out hope that the ship had found shelter from the storm somewhere and would soon be located; others wondered if any *Fitzgerald* survivors were in the freezing water, awaiting rescue and struggling to stay alive.

It was about 2 a.m. on Tuesday, November 11, when the *Anderson* and her exhausted crew arrived back on the search scene, joined a short while later by the *William Clay Ford*. Two Coast Guard aircraft were already circling above, lighting up the area with their searchlights. The HU-16 fixed wing had been the first on the scene, arriving at 10:53 p.m.; the HH-52 helicopter with the Nightsun searchlight had arrived two hours later.

At around 3 a.m., other vessels began to arrive on the scene. They had adjusted their speeds and routes in response to the call from the Coast Guard. Among them were the lake freighters *Wilfred K. Skyes, Roger Blough, Armco, Reserve, William R. Roesch, Frontenac,* and *Joan A. McKellar,* and the fishing boat *James D.* As the ships searched the site, more planes arrived, including two C-130 Hercules from CFBT and the Michigan Air National Guard.

For aircraft and vessels alike it was a dangerous search-and-rescue mission, conducted under terrible conditions. Though the weather had let up slightly, the waves still slammed the ships. Meanwhile, aircrews battled strong winds as they fought to maintain control of their planes and keep the search area illuminated. The scene was surreal: shadowy ships were weaving eerily among bright beams of light that sliced through the dark skies.

As the sailors scrutinized the dark waters, they held on to a faint hope that they would find at least some of the 29 men from the *Fitzgerald.* Perhaps survivors would be bobbing in the water, strapped to their life jackets. Or perhaps some were clinging to a lifeboat or a scrap of debris. The sailors kept telling themselves it was possible. After all, rescuers had found two survivors after the *Bradley* had sunk, and a sole survivor, Dennis Hale, after the *Morrell* disaster.

Shortly after 8 a.m. on Tuesday morning, the *Anderson* spotted the first debris from the *Fitzgerald*— a piece of one of

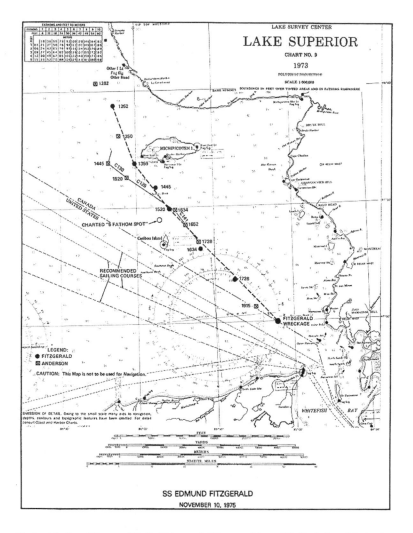

Probable tracklines of S.S. Edmund Fitzgerald *and* S.S. Arthur M. Anderson *on November 10, 1975. (From U.S. Coast Guard. National Transportation Safety Board. "Marine Accident Report. S. S. Edmund Fitzgerald Sinking in Lake Superior." Report # NTSB-MAR-78-3. May 4, 1978.)*

her lifeboats — floating nine miles east of the shipwreck site. Within an hour, another lifeboat was seen in the water about four miles from the first sighting. When the two lifeboats were later recovered around Coppermine Point, it was discovered that lifeboat number one was badly damaged, with its stern shorn off, while lifeboat number two was mangled but intact. Both were believed to have been unused, as they revealed no signs of survivors.

Onshore, nine Ontario Provincial Police (OPP) officers searched the rocky Lake Superior shoreline north of Pancake Bay, picking up some of the *Fitzgerald's* life belts and other small pieces of wreckage debris. Over the next few days, more flotsam was recovered and identified as belonging to the *Fitzgerald*, including 21 cork lifejackets, 8 oars or oar parts, 13 flotation tanks (from the lifeboats), 2 propane cylinders, and 13 life rings (with pieces of line attached).

Late on Tuesday, November 11, Lieutenant William Holt of the U.S. Coast Guard told reporters that nearly all of the life-saving equipment aboard the *Fitzgerald* had been recovered. However, no bodies had been found. "We're going to search for survivors for as long as we are able or until headquarters in Cleveland tell us to stop," Holt promised. He then added that it was possible that no bodies would ever be found, especially if the crew had been trapped inside the *Fitzgerald*.

As the search operation continued, a new concern began to emerge — oil pollution. The *Fitzgerald* had been carrying 72,000 gallons of thick Bunker C oil. Already two oil slicks had been reported, one of which was only 14 miles from shore. Officials, however, felt that the oil had already broken up in the rough water. Still, just in case more oil slicks were found, a joint Canadian-U.S. team stood ready to move into action. Ensign Jim Havermale from the U.S. Coast Guard commented that the cold water temperature at the lake's bottom had probably turned the oil into "one asphalt mess." He added, "If it stays in [the ship's] tanks it might be better to leave the oil there. If it is not leaking, then the oil has probably plugged the holes and sealed it in."

On Wednesday, November 12, two days after the sinking, a U.S. Navy plane, equipped with a magnetic anomaly detector, found what appeared to be the underwater wreck of the *Fitzgerald* about 17 miles north-northwest of Whitefish Point. The official search for survivors continued until just after 10 p.m. By the end of the search, there was no doubt in anyone's mind that the *Fitzgerald* had taken all 29 of her crew members to an icy grave.

Over the next three days, the Coast Guard cutter *Woodrush*, using side-scan sonar, located two large pieces of torn and twisted wreckage underwater on the Canadian side of the lake. However, due to weather conditions and the approaching winter, visual identification of the *Fitzgerald* would have to wait until the following spring.

End of an Era

A few days after the sinking, a memorial service for the *Fitzgerald's* crew was held at Detroit's Maritime Memorial Hall, at the mouth of the Toledo Harbor. Present at the ceremony was a frail, 80-year-old man, attending with his son. The elderly man was the ship's namesake, Edmund Fitzgerald, and his son, Edmund Bacon Fitzgerald (at the time the chairman/ CEO of Cutler-Hammer Inc. and chairman of the Milwaukee Braves baseball team).

The senior Fitzgerald had heard the tragic news of the sinking on the morning of November 11 while at his home in Milwaukee. His doctor and others had recommended that he not attend the memorial service, but he'd pleaded with his son to take him. As Edmund Jr. later recalled, "His mind was not as good as it used to be but he knew the ship went down. He felt terrible. He had a terrible feeling that with his name attached to the ship, he was somehow to blame."

The senior Edmund Fitzgerald died 11 years after the sinking, in 1986, but he never recovered from the loss of the *Fitzgerald* and her crew.

VI

What Happened to the *Fitzgerald*?

The sinking of the *Edmund Fitzgerald* left many burning questions. What had actually happened to the ship on the night of November 10, 1975? Had she broken in two on the lake's surface, like the *Bradley* and the *Morrell*, or had she broken upon hitting the bottom of the lake? Why hadn't McSorley or any of his officers sent out a distress call? Had a faulty ship design contributed to the disaster? Had there been any negligence, misconduct, or violation of law by the crew?

The U.S. Coast Guard quickly convened a formal Marine Board of Investigation to get some answers. At 10 a.m. on November 18, just eight days after the tragedy, the board began its inquiry in the Federal Building in Cleveland, Ohio. Comprised of Coast Guard members Rear Admiral Winifred W. Barrow (who served as chairman), Captain Adam S. Zabrinski, Captain James A. Wilson, and Commander C. S. Loosmore, the board was tasked with determining what had caused the sinking.

Captain Cooper of the *Arthur M. Anderson* was one of the first witnesses to be called to the stand and interrogated by

Rear Admiral Barrow. As part of the evidence, the board listened to a taped conversation between Cooper and four senior officials at U.S. Steel (the company for which Cooper worked). On November 11, after arriving back at Sault Ste. Marie following his search for the *Fitzgerald*, Cooper had called company headquarters in Cleveland to discuss what had happened: "He [the *Fitzgerald*] went in close to the island and I am positive in my own mind — we had him on radar — I am positive he went over the Six Fathom Bank."

Later in the same conversation, Cooper had said, "I know damn well he was in on that thirty-six-foot spot, and if he was in there, he must have taken some hell of a sea." Indeed, throughout the inquiry, Cooper was unequivocal in his belief that the *Fitzgerald* had gone over the Six Fathom Shoals north of Caribou Island.

In 12 days of testimony, between November 18 and December 13, the Marine Board heard 45 experts, studied 361 exhibits, and generated 3000 pages of proceeding documents. Nevertheless, it wasn't until the following May that the board received official confirmation that it was, indeed, the *Fitzgerald* at the bottom of Lake Superior. It was also at this time that the board was given a more thorough assessment of the freighter's condition.

Finding the Fitzgerald

In the spring of 1976, the Coast Guard cutter *Woodrush* returned to the wreckage site with the U.S. Navy's famous CURV III, a remotely operated underwater recovery vehicle. The CURV III had first come to the world's attention in 1966, when it recovered a lost hydrogen bomb that had fallen into the Mediterranean Sea following a collision between a U.S. Air Force B-52 bomber and its KC-135 refueling plane. Then, in September 1973, the CURV III had found itself in the international spotlight once again when it retrieved the Canadian-built submersible Pisces III and its two-man crew from the bottom of the Irish Sea, down 1375 feet. The two men had been stranded for three days and had only minutes of air left at the time of their rescue.

For the *Fitzgerald* expedition, the CURV III was equipped with a 35-millimeter camera system and two black-and-white television cameras. On May 20, 1976, those cameras gave the world its first look at the wreckage. Lying 535 feet down on the lake's bottom was the ship's stern, upside down and clearly showing the words, EDMUND FITZGERALD. It was the solid evidence needed to officially confirm the identity of the shipwreck.

The CURV III also gave investigators their first look at the ship's damage, and from the way the shipwreck was scattered on the lakebed, there was little doubt that it had been a catastrophic end for the *Fitzgerald* and her crew. Two huge pieces of the ship were embedded in mud, while the bow section was sitting upright, buried to about the same load line that the *Fitzgerald* had been sitting at in the water before she sank.

Judging from the appearance of the wreck, many theorized that the *Fitzgerald* had plunged to the lake's muddy bottom with such tremendous force that the impact had wrenched the ship in two while the stern — and the men trapped inside — was still on the surface. So violent was this force that about 200 feet of the *Fitzgerald's* middle section had disintegrated. Distorted, twisted metal debris was now scattered between the ship's two large sections. The stern appeared to have ripped away violently and perhaps circled the other half of the ship before coming to rest upside down, almost parallel to the bow but 170 feet away.

Between May 20 and 28, the CURV III made 12 dives to the *Fitzgerald*, recording more than 42,255 feet of video and taking 895 colour pictures. When some of the Coast Guard's images of the sunken *Fitzgerald* were later printed in newspapers worldwide, readers looked at the black-and-white photos and imagined the horror of being on board the vessel when she sank. One particularly haunting picture gave a grainy glimpse into the pilothouse through a shattered window and showed the cord dangling from the radiophone.

For over 18 months, the Marine Board gathered evidence, read reports, reviewed photographs and video, and studied the testimonies of mariners, Coast Guard members, and workers at the American Bureau of Shipping and the National Weather Service. Finally, the board's long awaited Marine Casualty Report was released. Titled "S. S. EDMUND FITZGERALD, O.N. 277347," it was dated April 15, 1977, and was approved on July 26, 1977, by Admiral O. W. Siler, commandant of the U.S. Coast Guard. In the report, the board outlined its view of the *Fitzgerald's* final minutes: "Finally as the storm reached its peak intensity, so much freeboard was lost that the bow pitched down and dove into the wall of water and the vessel was unable to recover. Within a matter of seconds, the cargo rushed forward, the bow plowed into the bottom of the lake, and the midships structure disintegrated, allowing the submerged stern section, now emptied of cargo, to roll over and override the other structure, finally coming to rest upsidedown atop the disintegrated middle portion of the ship."

The Marine Board cleared Captain McSorley and his crew of any negligence, criminal acts, or poor seamanship. As for the ship's list, the board speculated that it could have been caused by "localized hull structure failure," but maintained that investigators did not find evidence of any such fracture. The board also dismissed the idea that the ship had broken up on the surface before sinking.

And what about the topside damage to the vents and fence rails? The report offered three possible explanations: the damage could have occurred because of "light grounding or near grounding" on the shoals north of Caribou Island; because of a "floating object" striking the *Fitzgerald*; or because of some "unidentified object on board breaking away in the heavy seas." However, the Marine Board felt that the flooding from the loss of the two vents and some fence rail was not "serious enough, by itself, to cause the loss of the vessel."

Though the report dismissed shoaling as the cause for the *Fitzgerald* sinking, it did note that "the shoal area north of Caribou Island is not shown in sufficient detail on Lake Survey Chart No. 9 to indicate the extent of this hazard to navigation." The board knew that a survey conducted by the Canadian Hydrographic Service after the shipwreck identified an uncharted shoal that extended at least one mile farther into the lake than shown on the navigation maps. Some say the uncharted shoal, which was less than six fathoms deep, would have been close to the track taken by the *Fitzgerald* on November 10.

The most controversial section of the report was the part in which it blamed ineffective hatch covers for both the flooding and the sinking. The board concluded: "The most probable cause of the sinking of the *S.S. Edmund Fitzgerald* was the loss of buoyancy and stability, which resulted from massive flooding of the cargo hold. The flooding of the cargo hold took place through ineffective hatch closures as boarding seas rolled along the spar deck."

According to the Marine Board, as the weather and sea conditions deteriorated and put more water on the ship's deck, the water poured through the hatches into the cargo hold, flooding the inside of the ship. With the added tons of water weight in her hull, the *Fitzgerald* sank deeper in the water, struggling to stay afloat each time she dove into a wave. Finally, the battering seas were too much, and the ship plunged to the bottom of Lake Superior.

In his reviewing remarks, Admiral Siler agreed that "ineffective hatch closures" had caused the flooding that led to the sinking of the *Edmund Fitzgerald*. He added, "The sinking was so rapid and unexpected that no one was able to successfully abandon ship."

Fueling the Shipwreck Debate

Not surprisingly, the Marine Casualty Report was met with skepticism; the Great Lakes marine community challenged its findings. One of the strongest voices of opposition came from the Lake Carriers Association (LCA), an organization that represented 15 shipping companies operating a total of 135 vessels on the Great Lakes. In a letter dated September 16, 1977, and signed by association president Paul E. Trimble, the LCA clearly laid out where it stood: "The lake shipping industry, proud of its safety record through the years, completely rejects the Coast Guard theoretical cause of the FITZGERALD sinking."

The LCA maintained that flooding had occurred because of damage to the bottom of the ship, "caused by an external force, such as shoaling." The letter continued: "After the initial damage caused by shoaling, the vessel laboured in heavy quartering seas for three hours as it proceeded towards Whitefish Point ... As the vessel filled up gradually from the bottom to the point where its buoyancy was marginal, a large wave or series of heavy waves could have raised the stern, starting the bow's dive underwater, never to recover. Since the pilothouse was on the bow it would have gone under immediately, leaving no opportunity to alert the crew or radio for help."

The National Transportation Safety Board (NTSB) added to the controversy by issuing its own official Marine Accident Report on the *Fitzgerald* sinking. This report, dated May 4, 1978, agreed with much of the Marine Board's report, but there was one major difference: while the Marine Board claimed that the flooding (caused by the problematic hatch covers) had occurred over time, the NTSB concluded that the flooding had been catastrophically swift. Storm stresses, the NTSB maintained, had caused the "sudden massive flooding of the cargo hold due to collapse of one or more hatch covers." This flooding had been so rapid that the *Fitzgerald* had sunk before the crew could transmit a distress call.

Though the NTSB report (like that of the Marine Board) had dismissed shoaling as the cause of the wreck, NTSB board member Philip Hogue did not agree with that finding. He wrote a dissenting view, one that concurred with Captain Cooper and many other Great Lakes mariners.

Hogue believed the most likely cause of the *Fitzgerald's* sinking was "a shoaling which generated a list, the loss of two air vents and a fence wire. Secondarily, within a period of three to four hours, an undetected, progressive, massive flooding of the cargo hold resulted in a total loss of buoyancy from which, diving into a wall of water, the *Fitzgerald* never recovered."

The Coast Guard's Marine Board, the National Transportation Safety Board, and the Lake Carriers Association all agreed that there had been massive flooding on the *Fitzgerald* on November 10, but even with all the marine resources, modern technology, and expertise available to them at the time, they failed to agree on the reason for the flooding.

VII

More Questions than Answers

U pon the completion of the official investigations into the *Edmund Fitzgerald's* demise, privately funded expeditions began to bring in a diverse mix of marine experts, shipwreck hunters, and adventurers to peer at the wreckage. The era of *Fitzgerald* expeditions began in 1980, and it did not come to an end until 15 years later.

The Calypso *Expedition*

On Wednesday, September 24, 1980, a yellow mini-submarine named *Sou Coupe* (diving saucer) became the first manned submersible to visit the *Fitzgerald*. The sub was launched from the *Calypso*, an oceanographic research ship owned by sea explorer Jacques Cousteau. Sponsored by the Canadian National Film Board and the Cousteau Society, the *Calypso* Expedition was making a film about the natural history of the Great Lakes and the St. Lawrence River. Cousteau's son, Jean-Michel, led the expedition.

Calypso crew members were dealing with their own tragedy when they arrived at the *Fitzgerald* site. Just two weeks ear-

89

lier, one of their divers had lost his life in a diving accident on Lake Ontario. It had been the *Calypso's* first diving accident in 30 years, and it was still very much on everyone's mind as they prepared the *Sou Coupe* for the *Fitzgerald* dive.

Inside the squat mini-sub was the *Calypso's* captain and chief diver, Albert Falco, and French cinematographer Colin Mounier. Once the sub was launched, it did not take the pair long to locate the wreckage in the black waters below the surface of Lake Superior. As they moved toward the *Fitzgerald's* bow, a pale, eerie glow coming from one of the portholes gave the scene a ghostly look. Unnerved, Falco and Mounier soon recognized the light source — it was their own diving lights reflecting back from the glass.

The mini-sub drifted slowly around the shipwreck for the next 30 minutes while Mounier and Falco looked carefully at the *Fitzgerald*, filming as they went. After the dive, Jean-Michel Cousteau held a press conference in Sault Ste. Marie and announced that the two divers had found the bow section badly dented, as if something had banged it before it had sunk. Then came an unexpected conclusion from the Cousteau team: they believed the *Fitzgerald* had broken into two sections on the surface of Lake Superior and had subsequently sunk — slowly.

The team theorized that after the *Fitzgerald* had split in two on the heavy seas, the bow had struck the stern. Both sections had then floated for a while before slipping under the waves together. Cousteau insisted that if the *Fitzgerald* had broken in two and had sunk quickly, the bow would have been sitting farther away from the aft section.

Though investigating the reasons behind the *Fitzgerald's*

sinking had not been the main purpose of the *Calypso* Expedition, their conclusions were added to the many other *Fitzgerald* theories already circulating.

The ROV Expedition

It was August 1989 — nine years after the Cousteau team presented its findings — when the next expedition arrived at the shipwreck site. Organized by the Michigan Sea Grant Program at Michigan State University, the four-day ROV Expedition comprised experts from U.S. and Canadian organizations, including the National Geographic Society, the Royal Ontario Museum, the Michigan Department of Natural Resources, the National Oceanographic & Atmospheric Administration, the U.S. Army Corps, and the Great Lakes Shipwreck Museum. The team's plan was to launch a highly technological Remote Operated Vehicle (ROV) from its research support ship, the *R. V. Grayling*, in order to get a better look at the wreck.

Since the sinking of the *Fitzgerald* in 1975, most mariners had agreed that, because the ship had gone down so quickly (and without a distress call), no crew members had managed to escape. But the ROV discovered some haunting new evidence that challenged this long-held assumption: its colour video clearly showed an open port-side pilothouse door.

Why was this so significant? It seems that during a storm, all doors are dogged (locked) from the inside. For the pilothouse door to be open, McSorley or one of his officers must have deliberately unlocked the door before the *Fitzgerald* slammed into the muddy lake bottom. Had someone tried to escape from the pilothouse in those last horrifying moments?

Had he succeeded? And if one person had escaped, had others?

More Questions, but No Answers

The experts aboard the *R. V. Grayling* carefully scrutinized over five hours of video from the ROV. They examined the substantial damage to the bow and the extensive hull separation from the spar deck. They looked at the way the stern had settled almost parallel to the bow, and at the large amount of taconite pellets on the deck of the bow and scattered for hundreds of feet. And yet, they still could not discover the cause of the sinking of the *Fitzgerald*.

So far, each expedition to the *Fitzgerald* seemed to add a new layer of unanswered questions to the mystery of her wreck.

The MacInnis Expedition

From July 3 to 5, 1994, Dr. Joe MacInnis — a Canadian sea explorer, marine scientist, and author — led an international team of scientists on board the 168-foot research ship *Edwin A. Link* (owned by the Florida-based Harbor Branch Oceanographic Institute) to the wreck site. Called the "Great Lakes 94," this expedition consisted of a six-week environmental survey of the Great Lakes and St. Lawrence River. MacInnis had extensive experience in ocean exploration; he was the first person to dive under the North Pole, and one of the first to dive to the *Titanic* wreck.

The Great Lakes 94 Expedition used a 22-foot, three-person electric mini-submarine to explore and film the *Fitzgerald* wreck. Named the *Clelia*, the sub was owned by Harbor Branch and was similar in design to another of their subs, which, 21 years earlier, had become trapped on the sea floor near Key West, Florida, during a routine dive. As one rescue attempt after another failed, the sub's oxygen supply dropped and carbon dioxide levels climbed, turning the hull ice cold. At noon the next day, the sub was recovered, but the men inside were dead.

Following that tragic event, great strides were made in marine safety and rescue. In addition to the checklists and safety equipment that MacInnis's team had on board their research vessel, the Harbor Branch had equipped the ship with a remote-operated rescue vehicle that could reach the *Fitzgerald* in less than 10 minutes, in the event of an emergency.

The six dives by the *Clelia* — covering the bow and stern sections of the *Fitzgerald* and the debris in between — provided new information about the wreckage. It seemed the structural damage to the ship was much more severe than had previously been reported. However, the divers determined that the vessel's brass bell was in place and undamaged on the pilothouse roof, and that inside the pilothouse, the radar stand, water fountain, ship's wheel, and engine order telegraph were intact. A pile of debris had settled on top and below the chart table, and a black phone was visible, dangling beside one of the forward windows.

The divers could also see that the pilothouse telegraph was set at "full ahead," evidence perhaps that the freighter had been going at full power when she'd rammed through 25 to 27 feet of mud clay and made a 30-feet-deep trench on the lake floor.

After analyzing the expedition data and videotape from two cameras, the MacInnis team rejected the Cousteau theory from years earlier and concluded that the *Fitzgerald* could not have broken up on the surface of Lake Superior. And, as with all previous expeditions, no evidence of the crew was found.

The Shannon Expedition

The year 1994 was a busy one for *Fitzgerald* expeditions. Barely three weeks after the MacInnis group left the wreck site, another team arrived. This privately funded expedition was headed up by Michigan businessman Frederick J. Shannon, a scuba diver, former police officer, and *Fitzgerald* researcher/lecturer.

From the Canadian support ship *Anglian Lady* (a deepwater work tug contracted from Purvis Marine of Sault Ste. Marie, Ontario) the group launched a 16-foot, two-person research submarine equipped with still and video cameras. Called the *Delta*, the sub was owned by Delta Oceanographic of California.

It was on Tuesday, July 26, during their fourth dive, that Shannon's crew uncovered something no other expedition had found: a body wearing an orange life jacket. The body was lying in the mud on the port side of the pilothouse, near the open door, and its discovery prompted new questions about the *Fitzgerald's* final moments. Had McSorley had a chance to give the general order to abandon ship? Had the on-duty officers (McSorley, McCarthy, Cundy, and O'Brien) unlatched the pilothouse door and escaped? Or had the body drifted to the site from some other past shipwreck? No one could say for sure.

On his seventh and final dive, Shannon left behind a plaque with the names of the *Fitzgerald's* 29 crew members, as well as that of the late Captain Jesse Cooper (who had died in the spring of 1993 after retiring to Florida) and the participants of the Shannon expedition. The plaque was placed just aft of the pilothouse.

After careful study of his material, Shannon determined that the *Fitzgerald* had suffered "massive structural failure" and agreed with Cousteau that the ship had broken up on the surface of Lake Superior. He added the controversial notion that not all of the *Fitzgerald* was in Canadian waters.

Bringing Up the Fitzgerald Bell

The following July (1995), the Great Lakes Shipwreck Historical Society and its director, Tom Farnquist, spearheaded a recovery expedition to the *Fitzgerald* to bring back the freighter's bell for permanent display at their Whitefish Point museum. With letters of support from many of the families of the *Fitzgerald* crew, Farnquist and the historical society had obtained the required dive permit from the Ontario government, as well as formal permission to remove the bell.

A massive undertaking, the bell recovery expedition took 10 days of diving. The Canadian Forces Maritime Command (unofficially Canadian Navy) provided surface operational support with its 245-foot *HMCS Cormorant* (a diving support vessel with a crew of 90) and two submersibles, *SDL-1* and *Pisces IV.* Can-Dive Marine donated its crew and a Newt Suit Atmospheric Diving System. Sony Corporation donated the use of high definition video equipment. The National Geographic Society and its photographer, Emery Kristof, coordinated the filming of the bell's recovery for a movie. The Canadian tug *Anglian Lady* was once again called into service as the support ship. Joining the small armada of ships over the wreckage site was the 85-foot private yacht *Northlander* carrying family members of the *Fitzgerald's* lost crew; they had come to witness bringing up the bell.

On July 4, a lone deep diver, 37-year-old Bruce Fuoco, descended into the water wearing the bright yellow and silver Newt Suit, a state-of-the-art insulated atmosphere diving suit that permits deep-water dive operations without need for compression. Shattering the inky darkness were intense light beams from the two Canadian Navy mini-subs perched on the shipwreck's railings. The powerful lights were aimed at the roof of the *Fitzgerald's* pilothouse and at Fuoco. Using a special underwater torch, he cut the 200-pound solid brass bell — 21.5 inches in diameter — from the roof of the pilothouse. His every move was captured by cameras on board the Canadian mini-subs — the first high definition images ever taken in such deep water.

As his on-surface dive team aboard the *Anglian Lady* winched up the lift line, Fuoco brought the *Fitzgerald* bell and its stanchions to the surface. The next day, Fuoco returned to the wreck to install a replica brass bell — engraved with the words *Edmund Fitzgerald* and the names of all 29 men who had perished — on the pilothouse where the original bell had been mounted.

Because the wreck of the *Fitzgerald* was officially located in

Ontario waters, the legal owner of the recovered bell was the Province of Ontario. But in a special ceremony on July 7, Ontario's minister of intergovernmental affairs, Diane Cunningham, presented the bell to Michigan's secretary of state, who then presented it to relatives of the *Fitzgerald's* crew. Some of the families celebrated the bell's return, saying it brought a sense of closure to the tragedy, while a few felt the bell should have remained with the ship at the underwater gravesite.

After undergoing a few weeks of restoration at Michigan State University, the bell was sent to the Great Lakes Shipwreck Museum. On November 10, 1995, the 20th anniversary of the sinking, the bell was dedicated and placed on permanent exhibit. At the dedication ceremony, family members of the *Fitzgerald* crew tolled the bell 29 times. They were followed by Canadian singer Gordon Lightfoot, who rang the bell a final time in honour of all the mariners who had lost their lives at sea.

Touching the Fitzgerald

Six weeks after the *Fitzgerald's* bell was retrieved from the wreck, another remarkable expedition to the site took place. Two professional American divers, Terrence Tysall and Mike Zee, became the first people to scuba dive 530 feet down to the *Fitzgerald*. Zee was a diver from Chicago, while Tysall was a Florida-based diver and instructor, as well as founder of the Cambrian Foundation (an organization dedicated to undersea research, preservation, and exploration).

For years, Zee had talked about diving to the *Fitzgerald*; he made it his life's goal to visit the wreck site. Whenever Tysall saw Zee at a diving event, he would ask him, "Have you gone on the *Fitzgerald* dive yet? When are you guys going to do it? Set a date and do it."

Then, in the mid 1990s, Zee approached Tysall to scuba dive with him to the *Fitzgerald* wreck site. Tysall — who credits the influence of Gordon Lightfoot's song "The Wreck of the *Edmund Fitzgerald*" for his own interest in the *Fitzgerald* — welcomed the opportunity to embark on such an exciting dive.

No group had yet attempted to take on the intense pressure and cold of the Superior waters with just dry suits and air tanks. "It was a logistical challenge," recalled Tysall, "but the technology and training was available to safely visit the site and we could do it without needing millions of dollars. At the time, it would be the deepest dive ever attempted on the Great Lakes. But if I didn't think we could safely do it, we would not have even tried. No cave or rusty metal or reef is worth dying for."

Zee and Tysall put together a small team, including two in-water support divers, Ken Furman and Mauro Porcelli. Their support ship was the *R/V First On*, captained by Zee's business partner, Randy Sullivan of Lake Superior Dive Tours in Sault Ste. Marie, Ontario.

On September 1, 1995, as the sun shone brightly and a slight breeze blew from the west, the two men descended into the depths of Lake Superior face-to-face (in order to monitor each other for high pressure nervous syndrome) to visit the *Fitzgerald*. Tysall later described the dive: "When Mike and I first saw the *Fitzgerald*, our depth was 490 feet. We descended slowly to 530 feet. I illuminated the hull and superstructure with my light. Mike and I slowly made our way along the wreck, being careful not to disturb anything out of respect for the lost crewmen. These first glimpses of the *Fitzgerald* gave the feeling of extreme darkness, cold and isolation. Mike and I looked at each other, and then we gently gripped the ghostly rail with both hands. For the first time in almost 20 years, living hands were touching the *Edmund Fitzgerald*." Years later, Tysall still referred to that moment as "amazing."

After 12 minutes on the lake bottom, the pair began their long journey back to the surface. The total dive time was three hours, most of it in ascent. Zee and Tysall had planned to make one or two more dives to the *Fitzgerald*, each time staying progressively longer on the bottom, but they had to cancel the dives due to bad weather.

When they arrived on shore, Zee, Tysall, and the dive crew went to the Great Lakes Shipwreck Museum. They saw the original *Fitzgerald* bell on display and purchased a commissioned print of the *Fitzgerald* showing the ship in two pieces on the bottom of Lake Superior. "Each member signed the print and it is now hanging at the Cambrian Foundation office," said Tysall.

Why did the two men perform such a dangerous dive? As Tysall, who has dived many times for the U.S. Navy, explained, "There was no hidden agenda. No cowboy bravado. It was the challenge of proving it could be done, both logistically and physiologically. And at the site, we paid our respects."

Since the dive, Tysall has often thought of the *Fitzgerald*. "The mighty ship seems lonely in the cold dark water beneath Lake Superior. It's astonishing to think that an enormous ship like the *Fitzgerald* can be sunk by a storm on a lake."

The End of the Expeditions

In 1995, the families of the lost crew members began to lobby the Ontario government to ban further expeditions to the *Fitzgerald*. While most of these family members felt a sense of closure when the ship's bell was retrieved, as a group, they also felt strongly that any further dives to the wreck would be a desecration of a gravesite. They urged the Province of Ontario to prevent such dives by legislation. And in early 2006, Ontario consented.

Under the Ontario Heritage Act, a new regulation now limits access to three shipwrecks in the Canadian waters of the Great Lakes: the *Edmund Fitzgerald* in Lake Superior, and the wrecks of the *Hamilton* and the *Scourge* (sunk during the War of 1812) in Lake Ontario. Anyone wishing to dive to one of these sites, or operate research equipment near them, now requires a site-specific license, which is issued by the provincial government.

In announcing the protection of the three shipwrecks, Ontario's minister of culture, Madeline Meilleur, said, "With more than 500 shipwrecks discovered in Ontario's lakes, our province has some of the finest marine heritage resources in the world. The sites we have chosen for special protection are unique. We want to ensure that these fragile underwater sites — all of which contain human remains — are treated with care and respect."

The news was exactly what the relatives of the *Fitzgerald* crew had been waiting years to hear. "We are very pleased that the Province has recognized the *Edmund Fitzgerald* as an important heritage site. We are thankful that the site is protected from unauthorized visits, and we can now be at peace," wrote Ruth Hudson (mother of 22-year-old deckhand Bruce Hudson) and Cheryl Rozman (daughter of watchman Ransom Cuddy) in a joint statement that was included in the news release from the Ontario government.

Rozman was further quoted on the new legislation in an article appearing in the Thunder Bay *Chronicle-Journal.* "I can rest now, knowing that my Dad is safe … You don't go into a graveyard and dig graves open on land and disturb them, and you shouldn't be able to do it on water, either."

According to Michael Johnson, manager of Heritage Operations for the Ontario Ministry of Culture, obtaining a license for future explorations of the *Fitzgerald* or the other two protected wrecks will not be easy. Approval will only be given to expeditions that can provide serious justification for wanting to see the wrecks. Johnson added that the regulation "makes explicitly clear that we do not want sport divers visiting those vessels, or anyone doing unapproved surveys of any kind." For those who violate the ban, the potential fine can be a hefty $1 million.

VIII
The Making
of a Modern Legend

L ake Superior is rich with fascinating legends and
myths. From the phantom ships that roam the lake's
dark, deep waters, to the mysterious spirits that lurk
beneath the waves, these tales have captivated sailors and
landlubbers alike. The greatest of the lake's modern legends, of
course, is the sinking of the *Edmund Fitzgerald*, and many cred-
it its fame to Canadian singer/songwriter Gordon Lightfoot,
whose haunting ballad, "The Wreck of the *Edmund Fitzgerald*,"
is known around the world.

Lightfoot's song, however, was not the first one to be written about the *Fitzgerald* disaster. That honour goes to Dr. Charlie
Frederick, a former assistant professor at the University of
Minnesota, as well as a songwriter/musician and an environmental scientist. Frederick was working on some songs in his
home studio in Duluth on November 10, 1975, when he heard
a news bulletin that the *Fitzgerald* was in trouble and that
searches were underway to locate the ship. Within hours, he
began writing a country western ballad for the *Fitzgerald* crew,
which he titled "Twenty-Nine More Men."

Thirty years after the *Fitzgerald* sinking, Frederick recalled in a 2005 interview, "I wrote the song during the week the *Fitz* went down. New details were being added to the news accounts and I wanted to be sure I included as many details as I could."

Dr. Frederick's song was a hit in the American Midwest and received considerable national airtime. Many *Fitzgerald* family members heard about the song and wrote to Frederick requesting copies. Nevertheless, it was Lightfoot's ballad that brought worldwide attention to the shipwreck story, forever linking the ship to the song.

The sinking of the *Edmund Fitzgerald* also fuelled an enormous commercial enterprise. Since the tragedy, a variety of namesake souvenirs — including ball caps, t-shirts, coffee mugs, and paintings — have been produced and purchased eagerly; an opera has been written about the event; countless *Fitzgerald*-focused videos, books, and web sites have been created; and an English rock band has named itself after the doomed ship.

The commercialization of the *Fitzgerald* has a positive side because it has renewed interest in the somewhat-forgotten stories of other shipwrecks. Today, a new generation of young people has joined marine researchers, historians, shipwreck enthusiasts, and the general public in remembering the ships and crews that have sailed the Great Lakes.

Meanwhile, the legend of the *Fitzgerald* has taken on a somewhat unearthly aura, even among sailors. Some Great Lakes mariners tell of an unusually heightened awareness when sailing near the site of the *Fitzgerald* wreckage. A few, including Captain Erik Wood, have experienced eerie happenings. Wood's spine-tingling incident took place on a cold November night, when he was heading east for Sault Ste. Marie. He later recalled, "As we approached the general area of the *Fitzgerald*, the ship lost power. We drifted for what was probably less than 2–3 minutes ... and then like somebody flicked on a switch, the power came back online. When I did a fix on the position, we were about 300 yards east of the position of the *Fitzgerald* and as I was about to turn to the first mate, we heard rather a large gong ... like a bell ringing. We looked and I didn't see a thing. Radar showed nothing."

The chief engineer told Wood that he could not understand why their ship had lost power, nor could he say how the power had been restored. The sailors on board, however, had their own explanation for what had happened — the *Fitzgerald* crewmen had just reached out in greeting from their watery graves.

Strange things had occurred even at the time of the 1975 sinking. Among these occurrences was a haunting vision that appeared to a 55-year-old woman. The woman claimed to have seen the events of the disaster as they unfolded in "real" time. Following the tragedy, she wrote a letter to crew member Robert Rafferty's daughter, Pam Johnson. In the letter, and in subsequent conversations with Ms. Johnson, the woman said that on the evening of November 10 she had settled down to read the newspaper, but the paper had turned into a television screen that showed her a ship going down in the Great Lakes. She watched as a man dressed in black overalls and stocking cap went up the ship stairs, stepped onto the deck, and hung on to the railing before being swept away by a wave. The name she saw associated with the man was "Robert." The woman said it wasn't until the next morning that she heard the *Fitzgerald* had gone down.

Pamela Johnson knew her father was the only man aboard the *Fitzgerald* whose name was Robert. Did the woman who contacted her see something that actually happened? Or was this simply another titillating story to add to the ship's legend and lore? Pamela does not speculate as to the vision's accuracy, but she does say that, even today, she can't imagine her father passing away in the cold waters of Lake Superior. Instead, she chooses to believe that his death came about more peacefully: "I like to think my dad's last moments were warm, under the covers in bed ... and that when he realized what was happening, he ... died before he could freeze."

Without a doubt, Lake Superior was a terrible place to be on November 10, 1975, but there were other ships that sailed and survived the same storm that day. Why had the *Fitzgerald* been the one to go down? According to some, the *Fitzgerald* had ventured out on Lake Superior a wounded ship in need of repairs. Indeed, within days of her sinking, the seaworthiness of the freighter was being questioned in the media. On November 18, 1975, the *Thunder Bay Chronicle-Journal* reported that a lawsuit had been filed against the ship's operators, Oglebay Norton Company, on behalf of two widows of the *Fitzgerald* crew. The lawsuit charged that the ship had been "negligent in getting out into those waters this time of year with the kind of equipment it had."

The storm that raged the day the *Fitzgerald* went down was

intense and vicious, and today, some meteorologists believe it may have been a "perfect storm" scenario. Using 21st century technology, three meteorologists from the United States National Oceanic & Atmospheric Administration (NOAA) recently set out to determine the weather conditions during the storm of November 9–10, 1975. In particular, these scientists sought to discover what the weather and sea conditions were like in the specific area and at the specific time the *Fitzgerald* sank. What they found was chilling: the very worst marine conditions during the storm occurred for a short period of time in a small specific area of Lake Superior — and that location was "coincident with the time and location at which the ship *Edmund Fitzgerald* was lost." To make things even more deadly, the hurricane-force wind gusts and waves over 25 feet high came west across the lake and would have smashed the already wounded and listing *Fitzgerald* broadside.

Lake Superior's perfect storm window was small in location and duration, but it was big enough to swallow the *Fitzgerald*, an ailing ship in the wrong place at the wrong time.

If there had not been a wicked November storm, if the weather had been good, would the *Fitzgerald* have made the trip safely? Possibly. But even in good weather, with her weakened hull and sailing with less winter freeboard than she was designed for, the *Fitzgerald* was inviting disaster. The big difference, however, was that in good weather a lifeboat could have been lowered for the crew to escape the sinking ship.

Captain Erik Wood explained that sailing through a major storm on Lake Superior is "part skill and part luck." He added, "If the weather is particularly bad, and especially if you are loaded, you get even more tense. Your eyes watch the cargo deck. When you watch it flex and move in accordance with Mother Nature's wishes, you get an uneasy feeling. Got to always remember that you are never in control — Mother Nature is ... and if she wants your ship, she will take you."

On November 10, 1975, the luck part failed to get the *Fitzgerald* through the storm.

The *Fitzgerald* ships had spanned the various eras of Great Lakes shipping, from the days when sailing schooners and steamships were the main vessels on the open water, to the days of the first large lake freighters. There had been a *Fitzgerald* ship working almost every year on the Great Lakes for 105 years — until the sinking of the *Edmund Fitzgerald* on November 10, 1975.

When Mother Nature claimed the *Fitzgerald*, she ended the *Fitzgerald* era and started the *Fitzgerald* legend.

Epilogue

Every year on the Sunday closest to November 10, the historic Mariners' Church of Detroit (sometimes called The Maritime Sailors' Cathedral) is jam-packed with people. For 30 years, they were there for the *Edmund Fitzgerald* Memorial Service, commemorating the crew of the *Fitzgerald* and all other lost mariners of the Great Lakes. In 2006, the event was renamed the Great Lakes Memorial Service and dedicated to all mariners who sail the Great Lakes.

The roots of the traditional service reach back to the morning of November 11, 1975, the day after the *Fitzgerald* sank. Upon hearing the tragic news, the rector of the Mariner's Church, the late Bishop Richard W. Ingalls Sr. (who was a reverend at the time), went to his church, tolled the bell 29 times (one chime for each *Fitzgerald* crewmember), and then prayed for the men.

Since then, the church's congregation has held this annual memorial service, and they are joined by family members of the *Fitzgerald's* last crew, Great Lakes captains and mariners, and members of the general public. At the 1992 service, Captain James A. Wilson, a member of the U.S. Marine Board that investigated the sinking of the *Edmund Fitzgerald*, put into words the thoughts of many mariners

He said:

"Sailors are fortunate in the gifts they receive. They have a respect and love for their fellow seafarers unknown in other careers ... a respect that goes beyond the bounds of language ... they have a love for the sea, lakes and the oceans ... The sailor faces the everyday challenges of loneliness and separation. He faces the forces of nature ... and the insufferable heat of the engine room in midsummer ... finally there is a storm ... the one that tests the mettle and abilities of everyone involved ... the skill of the master ... the performance of the crew. The mariners present know that the Fitzgerald's storm could have been their storm."

On the 30th anniversary of the *Fitzgerald* tragedy (November 10, 2005), there still had not been a definitive report filed that explained unequivocally what caused the sinking of the *Fitzgerald*. And with each additional passing year, it seems less likely that there ever will be. But perhaps it's for the best: part of the lure of the *Fitzgerald* legend is the mystery of what really happened on the stormy night of November 10.

And what should the world remember about the *Edmund Fitzgerald*? Pamela Johnson was asked that question in 2005, and her answer was clear and strong: "Remember the good things about the crew ... and that the *Fitzgerald* was a beautiful ship."

Appendix A
Chronology of Events

November 9, 1975

8:30 a.m. Superior, Wisconsin: loading of taconite pellets begins on *Edmund Fitzgerald*.

2:52 p.m. *Edmund Fitzgerald* sails past Superior breakwall and out into Lake Superior.

3:30 p.m. Freighter *Arthur M. Anderson* backs out of Two Harbors, Minnesota and heads out into Lake Superior with load of taconite pellets for Gary, Indiana.

9:00 p.m. National Weather Service (NWS) issues a gale warning.

November 10, 1975

1:00 a.m. *Edmund Fitzgerald* is approximately 20 miles south of Isle Royale's Siskiwit Bay.

2:00 a.m. NWS upgrades gale warning to storm warning.

3:00 a.m. *Edmund Fitzgerald* passes *Arthur M. Anderson*.

7:00 a.m. Both *Edmund Fitzgerald* and *Arthur M. Anderson* sailing northeast.

9-10 a.m. Both ships change to eastward course, parallel to Ontario's north shore.

111

Noon to mid-afternoon Both ships on southeast course. Pass through the eye of the storm. *Edmund Fitzgerald* southwest of Michipicoten Island and 16 miles ahead of *Arthur M. Anderson.*

3:15 p.m. *Edmund Fitzgerald* sails around Caribou Island. Snow and sleet turn into blinding snowstorm.

3:30 p.m. Captain McSorley calls *Arthur M. Anderson* and reports topside damage, a list, "check down" and asks *Anderson* to stay by her.

4:00 p.m. Both ships in open water headed for Whitefish Bay. Pummeled by northwest winds.

5:45 p.m. Captain McSorley tells *Avafors* that *Edmund Fitzgerald* has "bad list."

7:10 p.m. *Arthur M. Anderson's* first mate talks to Captain McSorley – the last contact with *Edmund Fitzgerald.*

7:25 p.m. Snow squall stops. *Edmund Fitzgerald* has disappeared from radar and from visual sight while in Canadian waters of Lake Superior.

7:39 p.m. Captain Cooper makes first call to U.S. Coast Guard.

8:32 p.m. Captain Cooper talks again to U.S. Coast Guard, saying he is "very concerned."

9:03 p.m. Search and rescue operation launched by U.S. Coast Guard's Rescue Coordination Center. *Arthur M. Anderson*, now in Whitefish Bay, requested to assist in search, heads back out to the last known position of the *Fitzgerald.*

9:16 p.m. Canadian Forces Base Trenton advised.

9:25 p.m. U.S. Coast Guard harbor tug *Naugatuck* leaves Sault Ste. Marie (Michigan) for search scene.

9:30 p.m. U.S. Coast Guard *Woodrush* in Duluth is ordered to search site.

10:06 p.m. First rescue aircraft, a HU-16 fixed wing, leaves

Traverse City, Michigan. Meanwhile, U.S. Coast Guard asks other ships if they would go to search site to assist.

10:23 p.m. First Sikorsky HH-52 helicopter leaves Traverse City.

10:53 p.m. Fixed wing HU-16 arrives at search site. By now, media already reporting that the *Edmund Fitzgerald* is missing.

November 11

12:53 a.m. HH-52 Sikorsky helicopter arrives at search site.

2:00 a.m. *Arthur M. Anderson*, followed shortly by *William Clay Ford*, arrive at search site.

3:00 a.m. Other ships and planes arrive at search site.

8:00 a.m. *Arthur M. Anderson* spots first debris from *Edmund Fitzgerald*.

November 12

U.S. Navy plane, equipped with a magnetic anomaly detector, found what appeared to be the underwater wreck of the *Edmund Fitzgerald*.

10:00 p.m. Search for survivors of the *Edmund Fitzgerald* is discontinued.

Subsequent Events

1975: November 14-16: First side-scan sonar search with U.S. Coast Guard cutter *Woodrush* locates pieces of wreckage underwater.

November 18: At 10:00 a.m., Marine Board of Investigation into sinking begins inquiry in Cleveland, Ohio.

November 22-28: Second side-scan sonar search performed with *Woodrush.*

1976: **May 12-16:** Third side-scan sonar survey conducted.

May 20-28: U.S. Coast Guard cutter *Woodrush,* using CURV (cable-controlled underwater research vehicle) locate and photograph *Edmund Fitzgerald.*

1977: Marine Casualty Report released, dated April 15 and approved July 26.

September 16: Letter from Lake Carriers Association disputes findings of Marine Casualty Report.

1978: National Transportation Safety Board Marine Accident Report released, dated May 4.

1980: **September 24:** Jacques Cousteau's "Calypso Expedition" reaches *Edmund Fitzgerald* with manned submersible *Sou Coupe* (Diving Saucer).

1989: **August 23-26:** "ROV Expedition" organized by Michigan Sea Grant Program reaches *Edmund Fitzgerald* with remote operated vehicle (ROV).

1994: **July 3-5:** "Great Lakes 94" Expedition (MacInnis Expedition) backed by Harbor Branch Oceangraphic Institute makes extensive 3-day dive to wreck with electric mini-sub *Clelia.* Expedition's team of international scientists is led by Canadian explorer and marine scientist Dr. Joe MacInnnis.

July 26: "Shannon Expedition," privately-funded by Michigan businessman and *Fitzgerald* researcher/lecturer Frederick J. Shannon, uses research submarine *Delta* to reach the *Edmund Fitzgerald.*

1995: **July 4-5:** "Memorial 95" expedition removed the bell from the *Edmund Fitzgerald* with assistance of Canadian Forces Maritime Command's HMSC *Cormorant,* their two submersibles and deep sea diver Bruce Fuoco. The expedition's international major partners included Great Lakes Shipwreck Historical Society, Sault Tribe of the Chippewa

Indian Nation, Canadian Forces Maritime Command, *Anglian Lady*, Can-Dive Marine, Sony Corporation and National Geographic Society.

September 1: "Touching the *Fitzgerald*." American professional divers Terrence Tysall and Mike Zee scuba dive 530 feet to reach and touch the *Edmund Fitzgerald*.

November 10: The bell, removed from the *Edmund Fitzgerald*, is placed on permanent exhibition at the Great Lakes Shipwreck Museum, Whitefish Point, Michigan.

2006: Province of Ontario passes Ontario Heritage Act limiting access to three ships in Canadian waters, including the *Edmund Fitzgerald*.

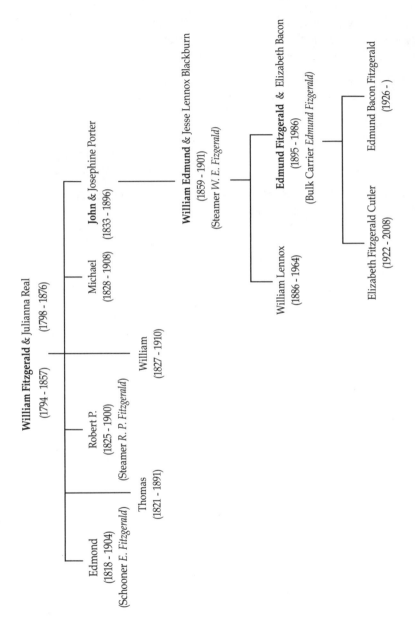

Appendix B. The family tree of the six Fitzgerald brothers who sailed the Great Lakes.

Bibliography

Bishop, Hugh E. and Captain Dudley Paquette. *The Night the Fitz Went Down*. Duluth: Lake Superior Port Cities Inc., 2000.

Brown, David G. *White Hurricane*. New York: McGraw Hill, 2004.

Cutler, Elizabeth F. and Walter M. Hirther. *Six Fitzgerald Brothers, Lake Captains All*. Milwaukee: Wisconsin Marine Historical Society, 1983.

Fitzgerald, Edmund Bacon. *Edmund Fitzgerald: The Ship and the Man*. Manitowish Waters, Wisconsin: Greer's Pier Books, 2001.

Hemmingway, Robert J. *Gales of November: The Sinking of the Edmund Fitzgerald*. Chicago: Contemporary Books Inc., 1981.

Hultquist, Thomas R., Michael R. Dutter, and David J. Schwab. "Re-examination of the 9–10 November 1975 Edmund Fitzgerald Storm Using Today's Technology," *Bulletin of the American Meteorological Society 2006, 87: 607-622*.

MacInnis, Dr. Joseph. *Fitzgerald's Storm: The Wreck of the Edmund Fitzgerald*. Holt, Michigan: Thunder Bay Press, 1998.

Nute, Grace Lee. *Lake Superior*. New York and Indianapolis: Bobbs Merrill, 1944.

Ratigan, William. *Great Lakes Shipwrecks and Survivals*. Grand Rapids, Michigan: Wm. B. Eerdmans Publishing Company, 1977.

Spring, Barbara. *The Dynamic Great Lakes*. Baltimore: America House Book Publishers, 2001.

Stonehouse, Frederick. *The Wreck of the Edmund Fitzgerald*. Gwinn, Michigan: Avery Color Studies, 1998.

Unwin, Peter. *The Wolf's Head: Writing Lake Superior.* Toronto: Viking Canada, 2003.

U.S. Coast Guard. "Commandant's Action on Marine Board of Investigation: foundering of the S.S. Carl D. Bradley, Lake Michigan. 18 November 1958 with loss of life." July 7, 1959.

U.S. Coast Guard. National Transportation Safety Board. *Marine Accident Report. S. S. Edmund Fitzgerald Sinking in Lake Superior.* Report # NTSB-MAR-78-3. May 4, 1978.

U.S. Department of Transportation. "Marine Casualty Reports. S. S. Edmund Fitzgerald; Sinking in Lake Superior on 10 November 1975 with Loss of Life, U.S. Coast Guard Marine Board of Investigation Report and Commandant's Action." July 26, 1977.

Wrigley, Ronald. *Shipwrecked: Vessels That Met Tragedy on Northern Lake Superior.* Cobalt, Ontario: Highway Book Shop, 1985.

Acknowledgments

A dedicated global community of people have generously contributed their talents, stories, and expertise to this book project. They have answered my questions, engaged in discussions, and, when needed, guided me in the right direction for additional resources and contacts. I am forever grateful for their support and assistance. They include, in alphabetical order: David G. Brown (author of *White Hurricane*); Edmund Bacon Fitzgerald; Dr. Charlie Frederick; Captain John Gilbert; William Hryb; Pamela Johnson (the daughter of *Fitzgerald* crew member Robert Rafferty); Captain Bud Robinson (special recognition to Captain Robinson for the dramatic painting of the *Edmund Fitzgerald* struggling in the November 10 storm and allowing it to be used on the cover of this book, and for the painting of the *Arthur M. Anderson*); Terrence Tysall; and Captain Erik Wood.

Index